IRAQ'S FUTURE:
The aftermath of regime change

Toby Dodge

ADELPHI PAPER 372

FIRST PUBLISHED MARCH 2005
BY **Routledge**
4 PARK SQUARE, MILTON PARK, ABINGDON, OXON, OX14 4RN
FOR **The International Institute for Strategic Studies**
ARUNDEL HOUSE, 13–15 ARUNDEL STREET, TEMPLE PLACE, LONDON, WC2R 3DX
WWW.IISS.ORG

Simultaneously published in the USA and Canada
by **Routledge**
270 MADISON AVE., NEW YORK, NY 10016

Routledge is an imprint of the Taylor & Francis Group

© 2005 THE INTERNATIONAL INSTITUTE FOR STRATEGIC STUDIES

DIRECTOR John Chipman
EDITOR Tim Huxley
MANAGER FOR EDITORIAL SERVICES Ayse Abdullah
COPY EDITOR Matthew Foley
PRODUCTION Jesse Simon
COVER IMAGE Mirrorpix/Getty Images

TYPESET BY Techset Composition Ltd, Salisbury, Wiltshire
PRINTED AND BOUND IN GREAT BRITAIN BY Bell & Bain Ltd, Thornliebank, Glasgow

British Library Cataloguing in Publication Data
A catalogue record for this book is available from the British Library

Library of Congress Cataloguing in Publication Data

ISBN 0-415-36389-6
ISSN 0567-932X

Contents

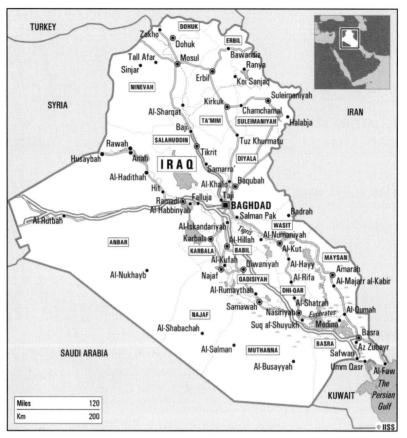

IRAQ (showing major settlements)

Glossary

CPA	Coalition Provisional Authority
ICDC	Iraqi Civil Defence Corps
IGC	Iraqi Governing Council
INA	Iraqi National Accord
INC	Iraqi National Congress
KDP	Kurdish Democratic Party
ORHA	Office of Reconstruction and Humanitarian Assistance
PUK	Patriotic Union of Kurdistan
SCIRI	Supreme Council for the Islamic Revolution in Iraq

What is at stake in Iraq?

It is hard to over-estimate what is at stake in Iraq. The removal of Saddam Hussein has proved to be the beginning of a long and highly uncertain process of occupation and state-building. For the Bush administration, a combination of ideological vigour, insufficient planning and misperceptions about Iraqi society has meant that the aftermath of war has been far more troublesome than regime change itself. The lawlessness and looting that greeted the seizure of Baghdad on 9 April 2003 has evolved into an organised, self-sustaining and politically motivated insurgency.

Against this background, the failure of American attempts to replace Saddam's regime with a stable, sustainable and hopefully liberal government will have major consequences far beyond Iraq, the region or indeed the United States itself. The aftermath of the invasion has important ramifications for the projection of American power. If the US is seen to fail in Iraq, then its foreign policy will have to be rethought and restructured. An unstable or anti-American Iraq would act as a potent symbol, highlighting the limits of US power and the dangers of intervening in rogue states.

For the Bush administration, regime change in Iraq was inextricably linked to al-Qaeda's assaults on New York and Washington, and became the lynchpin of a new and highly ambitious approach to foreign policy. The attacks of September 2001 gave Americans a heightened sense of their own collective vulnerability.[1] In their aftermath, the Bush administration strove successfully to convince the US electorate that the unilateral deployment of America's military dominance was necessary to combat this new form of asymmetrical warfare. Following the 11 September attacks, the administration was divided about how to approach the war against terrorism. Leading hawks, most notably Vice-President Richard Cheney and Secretary of Defense Donald Rumsfeld, made a strong case for the broadest possible definition of terrorism. This went well beyond the immediate hunt for al-Qaeda, placing the fight against terrorism at the heart of an ambitious new policy to transform international relations.[2] Although President George W. Bush was initially reluctant to do this, by the time of the State of the Union Address on 29 January 2002 the definition of terrorism had come to include not only the transnational networks of al-Qaeda, but also a series of states that had long posed a problem for US foreign policy. The 'axis of evil' facing America had become Iraq, Iran and North Korea 'and their terrorist allies'. These three rogue states were described as a grave and growing danger, not only because they were 'seeking weapons of mass destruction', but also because they 'could provide arms to terrorists, giving them the means to match their hatred'.[3]

In the 2002 State of the Union Address, and then more clearly in *The National Security Strategy of the United States*, published in September of that year, the issues of rogue states, weapons of mass destruction and terrorism had been forged into one homogenous threat to the security of the American people.[4] The dangers of instability and violence were seen to come primarily from the periphery of the international system. Bush's new 'grand strategy' located these threats in states in the developing world. These states' 'right' to sovereignty was now only to be granted when they had met their 'responsibilities' to the international community.[5] These responsibilities concerned the suppression of all terrorist activity on their territory, transparent banking and trade arrangements, and the disavowal of weapons of mass destruction. All necessary means, diplomatic, financial and military, were to be deployed to convince the ruling élites of errant states that it was in their interests to meet these new demands. However, this new doctrine faced two types of problem states, the 'failed' and the 'rogue': those that were either too weak to impose new responsibilities on their populations, and those that simply refused to be coerced.

For the Bush administration, as it set about applying its new doctrine in the aftermath of 9/11, the Ba'athist regime in Baghdad provided the vehicle for uniting the apparently disparate problems of terrorism, weapons of mass destruction and the need for 'offensive defence'. In the years that followed the invasion of Kuwait in 1990, Saddam's regime had become a potent symbol of a defiant Third World state. Throughout the 1990s, despite a partial invasion, continuous bombing and the harshest sanctions ever imposed on a country, it had steadfastly rejected the demands of the US and the international community. It was a powerful example for those governing élites of a rebellious disposition that state autonomy could be defended in a world dominated by the United States. By engineering regime change in Baghdad, Washington was setting out to signal its commitment to the Bush doctrine, as well as the lengths it would go to achieve its core foreign-policy goals.[6]

For the US government, regime change in Baghdad was to be the key that unlocked the whole of the Middle East. After 9/11 the Bush administration's attentions had focused not only specifically on Iraq, but also on the wider Middle Eastern region. The majority of states in the area had proved immune to the spread of democracy and free-market economics that had greeted the end of the Cold War. The 'Washington Consensus', the economic liberalisation imposed by the World Bank and International Monetary Fund in the 1990s, had little impact in the Middle East, and certainly did not cause any significant political liberalisation.[7] Bush directly linked the growth of terrorism facing the United States to the lack of democracy and economic development in the Middle East. In the run-up to the invasion of Iraq, he made it clear that the United States was no longer to be seen as a status-quo power in the region. A new and liberal Iraq was meant to act as an example to both the states and societies of the Middle East. To quote the president: 'A new regime in Iraq would serve as a dramatic and inspiring example of freedom for other nations in the region'.[8]

However, the size of the task involved in regime change in Iraq was not apparent to those in Washington who launched it. With the military capacity available to the United States, removing Saddam's ruling élite was certainly possible. But stabilising the governing structures in the war's aftermath, and then imposing sustainable political reform, was a much more complex and difficult task. Although military intervention into failed or rogue states has become increasingly common since the end of the Cold War, it has to date been largely unsuccessful.[9] The two definitive reports on international intervention take many hundreds of pages to say how the process should be carried out with greater technocratic efficiency, without detailing how government institutions can be built and, more importantly, how they can gain acceptance among the populations they are meant to rule.[10] The evidence is hardly inspiring. The United Nations Transitional Authority in Cambodia in 1992–93, the first large-scale UN attempt at root-and-branch political reform, failed to deliver meaningful change.[11] Intervention in Somalia resulted in 1994 in the ignominious exit of US troops and the collapse of the UN mission. Direct military intervention in Haiti to facilitate regime change in 1994 achieved nothing to alter the underlying politics of that country, as violent instability in 2004 highlighted. In Bosnia, Kosovo and Afghanistan, the mixed outcomes of intervention mean that it is too early to draw any firm or positive conclusions about the lasting successes or failures of these missions.

Failure in Iraq would also be very problematic for neighbouring states in the Middle East. Iraq's importance to the stability of the Gulf and the wider Middle East area cannot be overestimated. Geographically, it sits on the eastern flank of the Arab Middle East, with Turkey and Iran as neighbours. With a population estimated by the World Bank in 2004 at 27.1 million, it has a greater demographic weight than any of the bordering Arab states. With oil reserves second only to Saudi Arabia, its economic importance is clearly global.

In the late 1970s, after Saddam consolidated his domestic power, he used Iraq's geographical position, its relatively large population and its oil wealth to try and dominate inter-Arab relations. Over the next three decades, the country acted as a font of regional instability. If the present domestic situation does not stabilise, then violence and political unrest can be expected to spread across Iraq's long and porous borders. A violently unstable Iraq, bridging the *mashreq*, the most populous area of the Middle East and the oil-rich Gulf, would further weaken the fragile stability of surrounding states. Iraq's role as a magnet for radical Islamists eager to fight US troops on Middle Eastern soil would only increase. In addition, there is a strong possibility that neighbouring states will be drawn into the country, competing for influence and using proxies to further their own interests.

The success or failure of the ambitious aims brought together in the Bush doctrine depends on the effects of regime change in Iraq. If successful, it could at its most ambitious result in the projection of a coherent model for post-Cold War international relations across the world. However, one of the ramifications of failure could be the reduction of America's international ambitions and a change in the way it projects its power overseas. In addition, regional instability would increase and radical Islamic groups would be emboldened by the successful deployment of violence.

CHAPTER ONE

Order and violence in post-Saddam Iraq

The heart of any definition of state capacity is the state's ability to impose order on its population, to monopolise the means of collective violence across the whole of its territory.[1] Previous best practice from post-Cold War peace-keeping operations highlights the 'security vacuum that has confronted virtually every transitional administration-type operation'.[2] It stresses that establishing law and order within the first six to 12 weeks of any occupation is crucial for the credibility and legitimacy of the occupiers. For military occu-pation to be successful, the population has to be overawed by both the scale and the commitment of the occupiers. The speed with which US and coalition forces removed Saddam's regime certainly impressed the Iraqi population. In the immediate aftermath of Baghdad's fall, there was little doubt that US military superiority appeared absolute. However, the US military has been unable to impose and guarantee order across Iraq. This security vacuum has undermined the initial impression of American omnipotence, and has done most to erode coalition legitimacy and attempts at state-building.

What began in April 2003 as a lawless celebration of the demise of Sadd-am's regime grew into three weeks of uncontrolled looting and violence. To Baghdad's residents, coalition forces appeared unable or unwilling to curtail the violence that swept across the city.[3] The growing perception among Iraqis that US troops were not in full control of the situation helped turn crimi-nal violence and looting into an organised and politically motivated insur-gency. Former members of the security services, Ba'ath Party loyalists and those close to Saddam's family regrouped as the occupation failed to impose order. Taking advantage of the coalition's vulnerability, they began to launch hit-and-run attacks on US troops, with increasing frequency and skill. This security vacuum is the first and most difficult problem the new Iraqi administration will be judged upon. It is highly doubtful that it can succeed where the collective forces of the world's sole remaining superpower failed.

Troop numbers, whether American, coalition or indigenous, are one of the central problems facing the occupying authorities in Iraq. In a Senate hearing in February 2003, in the run-up to war, US Army Chief of Staff Eric Shinseki called for 'something in the order of several hundred thousand soldiers'. A widely cited study on state-building published just after the invasion concluded that occupying forces would need 20 security personnel, both police and troops, per thousand people. This compares to the 43 per 1,000 that sustained Saddam in power.[4] This means that coalition forces should have had between 400,000 and 500,000 soldiers to impose order on Iraq.[5] Instead, the US had 116,000 soldiers in Iraq in the middle of the invasion, with 310,000 personnel in the theatre as a whole. At the peak of their post-war deployment, following the elections in January 2005, the figure was 155,000.[6] These numbers demonstrate how fast and how far the Iraqi government has to travel to secure domestic law and order.

The difficulties in establishing law and order in the aftermath of the war have their roots in the type of campaign that US planners thought they were going to fight, and the type of resistance they assumed they would meet. There is strong evidence that the planners underestimated the resistance the invasion would face, not only by Iraq's élite regiments, the Special Republican Guard and the Republican Guard, but also by the mainstream army and the 30,000-strong irregular forces, most notably the *Fedayeen* Saddam and the Arab fighters who came to defend the regime from the US invasion.

In the first instance, advisers to the US government were working on the assumption that, at the advent of the air war or in the immediate aftermath of the invasion, an uprising or coup would remove Saddam from power and leave governing structures largely in place.[7] In an eve of war speech, Bush actively encouraged the Iraqi armed forces to move against their leaders.[8] Senior government sources in London were also looking for 'a political outcome, an implosion of Iraqi power from within, as opposed to an industrial strength war'.[9] If a coup failed to materialise, then the working assumption was that Iraqi forces would collapse or simply refuse to fight, in a similar fashion to the 1990–91 Gulf War, with thousands surrendering to allied forces.[10]

However, it was the wider strategic aspirations held by senior civilians at the Pentagon that played a key role in limiting the number of troops available to US commanders in Iraq. As part of his commitment to a 'revolution in military affairs', Rumsfeld put great emphasis on the use of precision bombing and technological advantage to limit the number of soldiers sent to Iraq. From as early as November 2001, Rumsfeld was encouraging General Tommy Franks, the man responsible for drawing up the plans for the invasion, to keep troop numbers as low as possible.

The reality of the war and its aftermath differed from the assumptions that underpinned the planning of the invasion. Sections of the mainstream army fought more tenaciously than many had expected. The level of Iraqi resistance in the south of the country, especially around Umm Qasr and Nasiriyah, surprised US Central Command, Iraqi analysts and possibly even the Ba'athist government in Baghdad.[11] There were two possible reasons why the regular army in the south fought much harder than expected, one organisational, the other ideological. Organisationally, Iraqi command and control had been delegated from Baghdad down to the level of each town. This meant that local commanders had been given executive power to run the battle in the best way that they could.[12] Supported by stockpiles of weapons and ammunition, this tactic encouraged the use of irregular forces, who were in turn bolstered by *Fedayeen* Saddam deployed from the centre. The second reason for the resistance continues to dominate Iraq: nationalism. There is no doubt that ordinary conscript soldiers, 80% of whom were Shia Muslims, hated Saddam, but there is nonetheless a militant Iraqi nationalism, born of three wars in the last 20 years and over a decade of sanctions. This was rallied during the war to motivate troops to fight against US forces with more tenacity than in 1990–91.

The evolution of the insurgency: tactics and targets

The insurgency is not homogenous in command and control, in personnel or in strategy. Clearly, US troops initially formed the main target, especially where they were at their most vulnerable, along supply lines and during troop transportation. But as US troops were redeployed to decrease their vulnerability and political visibility, the insurgents increased their targeting of Iraqis who were serving with fledgling state institutions. In addition, a small minority of those perpetrating the violence have deliberately targeted international institutions, specifically foreign embassies, the United Nations and the Red Cross, signalling that they would try and make any multilateralisation of the occupation both costly and unworkable. Finally, to encourage sectarian tensions radical Sunni *jihadists* have targeted high-profile Shia and Kurdish political figures.

The organisation of a low-level military campaign against US forces proved to be comparatively straightforward. The collapse of Saddam's regime allowed thousands of Iraqi troops to make their own way home. Untroubled by a managed demobilisation or disarmament, they simply merged back into their own communities. The stockpiling of weapons by the Ba'athist regime in numerous dumps across the country provided supplies of small arms and explosives. Historically, private gun owner-ship in Iraq has been comparatively widespread, and the majority of adult males have received some type of military training, with a large minority having seen active service. Saddam's regime never attempted to disarm the general population. The rapid collapse of the regime allowed munitions to become widely available at very low prices.

These factors combined with popular disenchantment with the occupa-tion to fuel the increase in politically motivated violence. Small bands of highly mobile assailants, making use of their local knowledge, inflicted increasing fatalities on US troops. With its genesis in late May 2003, by July the insurgency was beginning to show signs of greater professionalism, deploying organised reconnaissance to attack with maximum efficiency and minimum loss of life.[13] Capitalising on the US lack of armoured trans-port, the insurgents used Russian-designed rocket-propelled grenades and improvised roadside bombs to great effect. By July 2003, road travel for US convoys had become very dangerous. By October, US forces had recog-nised the increased geographical spread of the insurgency, better coordi-nation between the different groups and also their use of a wider range of arms, including mortars and mines.[14] The downing of several US army helicopters in the first two weeks of November 2003 further indicated the vulnerability of US forces on the move. Increasing US casualties gave the impression that the insurgents could strike with impunity. In addition, the growing violence encouraged a deep sense of insecurity in the wider population of Iraq, in turn increasing resentment against the occupation.

Since August 2003, car bombs have become a major part of the insur-gency. Attacks were initially directed at international targets to deter organi-sations and states that might have come to the United States' aid. A crude car bomb blew up outside the Jordanian embassy on 7 August 2003, kill-ing 17 people and injuring 50. The Jordanian government had supported the invasion, and the targeting of its embassy appeared designed to warn against further involvement. On 19 August a lorry packed with over 1,000lb of explosives blew up below the office window of Sergio Vieira de Mello, the United Nations special representative in Baghdad, killing him and 22 members of his team. Vieira de Mello's murder was a deliberate attempt by the radical fringe of the insurgency to prevent the internationalisation of Iraq's reconstruction. At the end of October, the Baghdad offices of the International Committee of the Red Cross were targeted. The cumulative effect of these attacks was to isolate Iraq further from the international community, forcing the United Nations and other agencies to scale down their presence in the country or to relocate to Jordan. By late 2004, car bomb attacks were taking place almost daily: in September alone, 35 car bombs exploded, the vast majority of them detonated by suicide bombers.[15]

As US troops were redeployed to more secure bases outside urban areas, the insurgents sought more accessible targets in the nascent institutions and personnel of the new Iraqi state. This change in tactics was heralded by an attack on three police stations in Baghdad on the same day in October 2003. Since then, car bombs have been used against police stations and army recruiting centres across the south and centre of the country. These attacks were exemplified by a devastating suicide car bomb assault at the end of February 2005 on an army recruiting centre in Hillah, a town 100 km south-east of Baghdad; at least 115 people were killed. Such attacks are designed not only to discourage Iraqis from working for the new state, but also to stop the growth of its institutions. They undermine attempts to deliver to the Iraqi population what they have been demanding since the fall of the Ba'athist regime: law and order. Between June 2004 and February 2005, an estimated 1,342 Iraqi soldiers and police were killed.[16]

Sectarian violence has the potential to be even more damaging to Iraq's long-term stability. In August 2003, a massive explosion outside the Imam Ali Mosque in Najaf (one of the holiest shrines of Shia Islam) killed some 100 people, including Ayatollah Mohammed Bakr al Hakim. Al Hakim was the leader of the Supreme Council for the Islamic Revolution in Iraq (SCIRI), one of several organisations claiming to represent Iraqi Shias, and a group that the UK and US had been courting to form the cornerstone of a new political order. The bombing not only signalled the high cost of becoming involved in the governance of Iraq, but also hinted at the increasingly sectarian nature of targeting. In February 2004 the tactic was extended to the Kurdish areas of Iraq, when two suicide bombers killed 101 people at the offices in Arbil of the main Kurdish parties the Kurdish Democratic Party (KDP) and the Patriotic Union of Kurdistan (PUK). Attacks in March 2004 targeted the large crowds that had gathered to commemorate the Shia festival of Ashura in Baghdad and Karbala, in a clear attempt to trigger a civil war between Iraq's different communities. This assumption was strengthened by the discovery in Baghdad of a letter allegedly written by a senior Islamist figure, the Jordanian Abu Musab al Zarqawi. This argued that the only way to 'prolong the duration of the fight between the infidels and us' is by 'dragging them into a sectarian war, this will awaken the sleepy Sunnis who are fearful of destruction and death at the hands of the Shia'.[17]

Iraqi politicians have blamed suicide bombings and the rise in sectarian violence on outside forces. But there is a danger that they have overstated their case.[18] The efficiency of these attacks, their regularity and the speed with which they were organised in the aftermath of Saddam's fall all point to a large degree of Iraqi involvement and direction. The organisation behind the sectarian attacks is much more likely to be a hybrid, with elements of the old regime acting in alliance with indigenous Islamic radicals and a small number of foreign fighters. This has allowed mid-ranking members of the old regime to deploy their training and weapons stockpiles. They have sought to ally themselves with a new brand of Islamic Iraqi nationalism, seeking to mobilise Sunni fears of Shia and Kurdish domination and a widespread resentment at foreign occupation. Although the use of indiscriminate violence has alienated the majority of Iraqi public opinion across all sections of society, the carnage it has produced has been a major setback for statebuilding and stability. Those deploying this form of violence believe that the resulting chaos will further de-legitimise the new Iraqi administration and hasten the departure of US troops. These groups believe they would be best placed to exploit the resulting political and security vacuum.

During the first weeks of April and again in August 2004, the insurgency took a new and dramatic direction. The Coalition Provisional Authority (CPA)'s decision to launch an attack on the radical Shia Muqtada al Sadr opened a second front in the opposition to occupation. Sadr, faced with an arrest warrant for murder, began a rebellion across the south of the country. Although his own forces numbered in the low thousands, other less wellorganised militias based in the south used Sadr's general call to arms as a cover to launch localised assaults on coalition forces. This upsurge in violence across the south coincided with *Operation Vigilant Resolve*, the US Marines' first sustained attempt to enforce CPA rule in Falluja. The result was to open two fronts of violent opposition to the occupation simultaneously. This undoubtedly bolstered the confidence of those organising the insurgency and allowed them to move from guerrilla warfare to open military confrontation.[19] Although the two insurgencies remained separated by geography and religious affiliation, there was evidence of limited tactical liaison between the two, sharing technical innovations and strategic advice.

The organisation of the insurgency
The evolving insurgency, involving diverse tactics and different targets, has several separate sources and a multitude of causes. The first group

comprises criminal gangs operating in and around Basra, Baghdad and Mosul. Organised crime accounts for 80% of the violence in Iraq.[20] These groups predate regime change, having come to prominence in the mid-1990s at the peak of the social and economic suffering caused by sanctions. Then, before the signing of the United Nations oil-for-food deal, Saddam's grip on society was at its weakest, and organised crime flourished. These groups have been revitalised by the lawlessness of present-day Iraq, the ready availability of weapons, the absence of an efficient police force and the CPA's lack of intelligence about Iraqi society. They terrorise what remains of the middle class, car-jacking, house-breaking and kidnapping, largely with impunity. Groups like these also regularly rob and kidnap foreign workers. In many cases, these gangs are better armed and organised than the Iraqi police trying to stop them. Their continued capacity to operate is the most visible sign of state weakness.

The remnants of the Ba'ath regime's security services constitute the second group involved in violence. This group is estimated to be responsible for up to 60% of the politically motivated violence in the country.[21] There are reports of extensive contingency planning carried out by Saddam's regime before the invasion.[22] The speed with which the government collapsed in the face of invasion and the chaos that collapse left in its wake mean that the initial evolution of the insurgency was reactive and highly localised. More influential in the upsurge of violence after regime change was the legacy that the Ba'athist regime left behind: a militarised society with a high degree of private gun ownership, widespread military training and experience of active duty.

Interviews conducted by the author with former regime loyalists in Baghdad in the spring and summer of 2003 suggest that the networks and personnel now pursuing the insurgency appear not to have been reconstituted according to pre-war planning, but instead through personal, family and geographic ties.[23] The decisions to dissolve the army and embark on root-and-branch de-Ba'athification in May 2003 contributed to the personal, face-to-face organisation of the insurgency by putting an estimated 750,000 people out of work.[24] Ba'athists interviewed in late May 2003 felt under attack and vulnerable. The CPA edicts, in conjunction with a spate of assassinations by radical Shia groups, forced them to regroup and reorganise.

Against this background, it was a small step for the Ba'ath Party, an organisation with a long history of covert operation, to move from reactively organising for self-defence to proactive offensive action. By November 2003, the Ba'athist arm of the resistance had begun to cohere. Documents seized by the US military when they took Saddam into custody in December 2003 indicated that he had been in regular contact with those organising the resistance. By 2004, a new politburo at the head of the Iraqi Ba'ath Party had been formed, with representation from both the civilian and military wings of the party, and with personnel resident in the country and outside.[25] The Ba'athist wing of the resistance is still highly localised and dependent upon personal and geographic ties for the majority of its organisational capacity. But there is clear evidence that the renewed covert organisational capacity of the Ba'athist underground is supplying finance and ideological encouragement to sections of the resistance.

The second factor supporting the insurgency is the coherence of the security networks that guaranteed Saddam's survival for so long. The 'Sunni triangle', the area of north-west Iraq above Baghdad, is often described as a homogeneous block of insurgency supporters, offering material and ideological comfort to the fighters. What is not understood is that Saddam's 'shadow state', with its flexible networks of patronage and violence, is still intact and functioning coherently in Iraq's north-west.[26] The same individuals who intimidated and demobilised Iraqi society in the 'Sunni triangle' remain there today. In and around Tikrit, violence is sustained by those closely associated with the inner élite of the old regime. But in other areas of the north-west, particularly in Baghdad, the insurgents have transcended the ties of the old regime and merged with a broader and more widespread revolt. In effect, the insurgency was 'de-Ba'athised' the day Saddam himself was arrested. It has diversified from its original ideological and organisational roots, and has now broadened its appeal to encompass both Islamism and nationalism.

The final source of violence is certainly the most worrying, and the hardest to deal with. This can be usefully characterised as Iraqi Islamism, with both Sunni and Shia variants. Iraqi political discourse has been strongly shaped by the twin ideological influences of Islam and nationalism: first Arab nationalism, but increasingly Iraqi nationalism. This has been the case since independence in 1932, but especially since the Ba'ath Party seized power in 1968.[27] After the 1990–91 Gulf War and the imposition of sanctions, Saddam infused the Ba'ath Party's long-established secular, broadly socialist rhetoric with an Islamism that reflected the Iraqi population's return to religion in the face of economic collapse and social dislocation.[28]

The strong nationalist and Islamic currents running through the Iraqi polity have created a political ideology that combines the defence of the *Watan*, the Iraqi homeland, with a war against foreign and non-Muslim invaders. A good example of this is the insurgent group, The Battalions of the 1920 Revolution. Formed in the suburban hinterland of Baghdad, this group has, as its name suggests, merged Iraqi nationalism with Islamic radicalism. In 2004, groups like this were the fastest-growing wing of the insurgency, responsible for up to 20% of the violence against the US military and Iraqi security forces. This ideological aspect to the resistance movement, with both Sunni and Shia adherents, is not going to disappear. The Interim Iraqi Government's attempts either to co-opt or marginalise this powerful ideological force were dependent on the extent to which the population saw the government as an authentic representation of society as a whole. With a high proportion of formerly exiled politicians in the cabinet and an interim prime minister, Ayad Allawi, closely associated with the intelligence arms of both the American and British governments, the indigenous nature of the government was very difficult to prove. The continued role of foreign advisers and security personnel in and around the seat of government, the heavily fortified 'green zone' in the centre of Baghdad, is a continuing problem for the legitimacy of the new government.[29] Allawi had very little in the way of resources or power to offer the regime's opponents; he found it difficult, for example, to draft an amnesty that would provide real incentives for fighters to lay down their weapons, while not falling foul of US sensibilities.

Muqtada al Sadr has been the political figure who has successfully rallied the nationalist and radical Islamic trends amongst Shia sections of the population. Sadr's support originates in the poorest and most disadvantaged sections of the Shia population. Capitalising on a large charitable network set up by his late father, Sadr has used radical anti-American rhetoric to rally disaffected Iraqis to his organisation. As the occupation forces failed to deliver significant improvements to people's lives, Sadr's popularity began to increase. In the run-up to the handover of power on 28 June 2004, Sadr's rhetoric and actions became more extreme in an attempt to convince the CPA that he could not be excluded from the post-occupation political settlement. Sadr deployed his own militia, the Mahdi Army, in al Tharwa, the large Shia slum in Baghdad (renamed Sadr City, after his late father, following regime change), and across the south of the country. The CPA responded by closing down Sadr's newspaper and arresting Sheikh Mustafa al Yacoubi, one of his key deputies in Najaf. The resulting revolts in key towns across the south of Iraq – Basra, Amara, Kut, Nasiriyah, Najaf, Kufa and Karbala – as well as in Baghdad itself showed that Sadr's organisation had been preparing for just such a confrontation from regime change onwards, and had been organising the Mahdi Army with this in mind.[30] Second, the geographic scale of the southern uprisings indicated that other, smaller militias and local armed groups were using Sadr's confrontation to launch their own strikes against coalition forces. The constituency that Sadr aspires to represent, the economically disadvantaged and politically alienated, will not disappear. The widespread casualties resulting from the suppression of the revolt, particularly in Baghdad, have created resentments that will take years to dissipate. Sadr, or politicians like him, will have continued access to a constituency large enough to fuel radical politics and question the legitimacy of the Iraqi government.

The final contributing factor in the insurgency is the most controversial and difficult to judge: the role played by Arab fighters from neighbouring countries, and behind them the organising capacity of al-Qaeda in Iraq. Paul Bremer, the American diplomat who acted as the civilian head of the CPA, and senior US military figures have stressed the crucial role of foreign fighters in general, and specifically al-Qaeda, in sustaining the revolt. Bremer has argued that al-Qaeda has infiltrated Iraq through its links to the Kurdish Islamist group Ansar al Islam. After the US overthrow of the Taliban in Afghanistan in 2001, Ansar's ranks were certainly augmented by al-Qaeda fighters.[31] However, Ansar was a small group with little popular support, the product of fractious Kurdish politics rather than widespread political mobilisation. In the run-up to the invasion of Iraq, its training bases in Iraqi Kurdistan were attacked by the PUK and the US Air Force. It is highly doubtful that a small Kurdish group with no history of operating outside Iraqi Kurdistan could rapidly reconstitute itself in and around Baghdad and organise a series of very effective car bombings in a matter of months.

The CPA has also presented the actions of the Jordanian Islamist Abu Musab al Zarqawi as evidence of a sustained al-Qaeda presence in Iraq. After the US invasion of Afghanistan, US intelligence placed him in Baghdad obtaining medical treatment and building up a base of operations.[32] Several of Zarqawi's assistants have been arrested in Iraq in 2004 and 2005, but to date little has come to light from their interrogation.

There is clear evidence of foreign fighters playing a role in the insurgency and the suicide bombings that have plagued Baghdad. Mobilised through diffuse and informal networks across the Middle East, they appear to have been making their way to Iraq in an uncoordinated fashion. However, their numbers appear to be comparatively low, estimated by the US Army to be between 500 and 2,000. In March 2004 fewer than 150 of the 10,000 security prisoners held by the US military in Iraq were non-Iraqi Arabs. Of the first 1,000 prisoners seized in the retaking of Fallujah, only 5% were foreigners. By January 2005, only 335 foreigners were being held by the US and Iraqi military.[33]

Although it may be politically expedient for American and Iraqi politicians to stress the non-Iraqi aspects of the insurgency, strategically the over-emphasis on foreign fighters may well undermine attempts to tackle the underlying causes of violence. Foreign fighters or radical Islamists are not the main or most important forces sustaining the insurgency. The revolt is very much a home-grown phenomenon, carried on by fighters from both the Sunni and Shia sections of society. The initial goodwill that greeted Baghdad's liberation has disappeared, and nationalist resentment has emerged in its place. While much of the initial violence was opportunistic, driven by criminal intent, and while Ba'athists and those close to the former regime certainly form part of the revolt, its mainstay is now much more widespread. Those fighting are doing so to rid their country of what they see as a foreign invader, and people they see as collaborators. The majority of the combatants have strong ideological reasons for opposing the occupation. If the Iraqi government fails to present itself as an indigenous, representative organisation, then the ideological motivation of the insurgents will continue to grow.

The problem of militias

The inability of occupation forces to impose order has given rise to a plethora of independent militias. These militias, increasingly organised along sectarian lines, have increased their power and visibility on the streets of Iraq's major towns and cities. The incoherent and partial application of CPA disarmament edicts, allowing Kurdish militias to retain their arms while demanding that certain Shia ones do not, has led to the militias filling the social void formally occupied by the security forces of central government. Although these militias enjoy little popular support, their existence is testament to the inability of the CPA and the Iraqi government to guarantee the personal safety of Iraqis.

The militias can be divided into three groups, depending on their organisational coherence and relation to national politics. The first group is made up of the two Kurdish militias of the KDP and PUK. These two separate forces number in total anything from 50,000 to 75,000 fighters. The Kurdish militias are the most organised, institutionalised and comparatively disciplined in the country. With a long history of fighting against the central government in Baghdad, the KDP and PUK quickly set about imposing order on their respective fighting forces once the United Nations had given their enclave protection in the aftermath of the 1991 Kurdish uprising. However, an extremely damaging civil war broke out between the two parties in the mid-1990s over control of the profits from oil smuggling. This had a highly detrimental effect on the governing structures of Iraqi Kurdistan. The two militias are still separate and still represent little more than the political ambitions of their two leaders.

The second set of militias are those that were organised in exile and brought back to Iraq in the wake of Saddam's fall. The most powerful of these are the Badr Brigades, the military arm of the Shia party SCIRI. The Badr Brigades, along with SCIRI itself, were set up as a foreign-policy vehicle for the Iranian government. Indeed, the Badr Brigades were trained and officered by the Iranian Revolutionary Guard, at least until their return to Iraq. Along with SCIRI, the majority of the formerly exiled parties have set up militias to provide security for their leaders, and to exert political and military influence. The final group of militias, and probably numerically the largest, are those that have been set up at a local, village or town level across Iraq. These are a direct response to lawlessness. They vary in size, organisation and discipline, from a few thugs with guns to militias capable of running a whole town.

In combination with the insurgency itself the militia fighters, conservatively estimated to number 100,000, pose the most serious threat to the long-term stability of the country. The nature of this problem has been recognised by the interim government and by the CPA before it. However, the negotiations surrounding the drafting of the interim Iraqi constitution and the Transitional Administrative Law avoided dealing directly with the militia problem. The law, finally agreed in March 2004, bans militias that are not directly controlled by the federal government, but adds the proviso that their members will be integrated into the government's security services or helped in making the transition to civilian life. As this process would necessarily take time, another contentious and potentially explosive issue has been set aside for the future. A second attempt to deal with the problem has been ongoing since March 2004, focusing on a disarmament, demobilisation and reintegration agreement. This culminated in Allawi announcing a deal on 7 June 2004 committing all the parties to demobilise their militias. This would involve 60% of their personnel being integrated into the new Iraqi security forces, with the rest being retrained for civilian jobs or pensioned off. The new deal immediately created two problems. First, the timetable for demobilisation will last until the end of 2005, leaving the majority of the party militias untouched for at least 12 months. Second, the PUK quickly announced that it was not included in the deal, as it had previously been given assurances by US and Iraqi officials that it could keep its forces intact. Adel Mirad, a senior PUK leader, claimed: 'The *peshmerga* are not included in this agreement. That is for the other militias. No change'.[34]

The Iraqi security forces

With a nationwide insurgency and facing militias numbering at least 100,000, US troops have clearly failed to impose order on Iraq. During the summer of 2004, the US embassy in Baghdad developed a strategy to defeat the rebellion in the run-up to the elections in January 2005. This was to have involved US forces bringing 20–30 key towns in the north-west of the country back under the control of the coalition and the Iraqi government before the election campaign started.

Samarra, a town of 200,000 people 105 km north Baghdad, was to be the first to be seized, with Falluja being the defining moment of the campaign.[35] Samarra was duly taken on 1 October 2004. Falluja came under sustained attack and then occupation on 8 November. However, the seizure of Falluja did not result in the pacification of the rest of north-western Iraq. The 'dynamic cordon' placed around the city by US Marines in the middle of October did not prevent large numbers of fighters leaving Falluja in the run-up to the well-publicised attack.[36] The campaign itself was greeted by an upsurge in violence across the whole of the region, with suicide bombings killing 39 people in Samarra. Mosul, with more than a million inhabitants Iraq's third-largest city, saw attacks on nine police stations and the desertion of 3,200 of the city's 4,000-strong police force. Although in public Lt-Gen. John F. Sattler, commander of the 1st Marine Expeditionary Force, hailed the Falluja operation a success, saying it had 'broken the back of the insurgency', a US intelligence report drawn up in the wake of the operation was less optimistic. It argued that the insurgency had shown 'outstanding resilience' and that, at current US force levels, 'the enemy would be able to maintain a sufficient level of intimidation of the Al Anbar and Babil Province populations and infiltrate or otherwise further degrade the capabilities' of the Iraqi government's security services.[37]

Longer-term plans for regaining control of the country concentrate on building up the capacity of the indigenous Iraqi security forces. In the run-up to the handover of sovereignty in June 2004, the US military focused on the creation of an army of 25,000 soldiers, in addition to a paramilitary guard of 51,000. This would represent a force a fifth the size of the army Saddam had at his disposal when deposed. Despite setting aside $1.8 billion for the task, the coalition had trouble raising and training this comparatively modest force. With the Falluja and Sadr revolts in April 2004, this new security force faced its first major challenge. Then, the Iraqi army consisted of two battalions. Up to half of the First Battalion resigned during training in December 2003, citing low pay and poor conditions. The Second Battalion refused to fight when pressed into service alongside US Marines during the siege of Falluja, arguing that they had joined the new army to fight Iraq's enemies, not Iraqis.[38]

To compensate for the slow pace of army recruitment and training, the Iraqi Civil Defence Corps (ICDC) was set up in late 2003. Much more *ad hoc* in its recruitment and training, the personnel for this force comprised an uneasy amalgamation of former employees of the old security forces, members of the militias formed by the political parties and those desperate for work.[39] A week before taking power in June 2004, Allawi announced that the ICDC, renamed the National Guard, would form the Iraqi government's main vehicle for enforcing order.[40] By October 2004 the National Guard had recruited 41,000 troops, still 20,000 short of its target.[41] The 36th Battalion of the National Guard has become the main striking force of the Iraqi armed forces, being deployed against the Mahdi Army in Najaf in August and Falluja in October 2004. However, this section of the Guard had been heavily recruited from the party militias of SCIRI, the KDP and PUK. The speed of this recruitment raises the issue of who these forces are loyal to: their parties or the new government. In addition, by recruiting so heavily from parties organised along sectarian and religious lines, this policy runs the distinct danger of introducing a divisive sectarianism into the armed forces. This, along with reports of senior Guard commanders being arrested for collaboration with the insurgents, highlights the problems of discipline and loyalty in a force so quickly recruited, trained and deployed.

Although Washington is committed to keeping 150,000 American troops in the country at least until 2007, all hopes of progress are now pinned on Iraqification. The aim is to quickly shift the burden of imposing law and order (and the cost in terms of lives lost) on to Iraqi forces. US army patrols, currently numbering over 12,000 a week, will be dramatically cut. Their place is to be taken by the Iraqi National Guard, army and police force. The US army will either be redeployed to less vulnerable roles or will act as 'mentors', stiffening the resolve of Iraqi forces by patrolling jointly with them.[42] The ambitious nature of this policy and the speed with which it is to be carried out raises the difficult question of how an army less than two years old is meant to succeed where US forces have made little headway.

The brunt of everyday law enforcement has fallen to the Iraqi police force. Relying heavily on personnel from the old force, recruitment and retention have been much more successful, with numbers estimated at between 73,000 and 92,000. However, training and equipment have been slow in coming. In mid-April 2004 it was estimated that only 13,000 had received training, and there have been constant complaints of poor equipment and scarce weaponry. When faced with political violence, police in many southern towns and in Falluja have either refused to fight, or in some cases have joined the insurgents. The focus on quantity rather than quality has meant that trainers have had very little time to instil standards of discipline and loyalty into the security force as a whole. Best estimates suggest that it will take up to five years to create anything close to an effective indigenous police force able to impose and guarantee order across the country.

Conclusions

The legacy left to the new Iraqi government by the occupation is daunting. It faces an insurgency estimated to be between 20,000- and 50,000-strong. These fighters are organised in as many as 50 independent cells, with a diffuse coordination between them.[43] With no coherent centre of gravity and no overall leadership the insurgency cannot be defeated simply by the application of force.[44] The new government elected in January 2005 does not have the capacity to replace US forces with the speed needed to turn the tide of the revolt. This dangerous interregnum, after occupation but before the birth of a credible Iraqi army, may eventually see the government controlling areas of Baghdad but little else.

Instead of focusing primarily on military solutions, the only option is to develop a coherent political strategy for combating the insurgency. This would involve listening to radical elements within both the Shia and Sunni communities, and ultimately integrating them politically, while at the same time demobilising them or at the very least limiting their capacity for violence. This will clearly be a difficult task, but the alternative military strategy has to date proved unsuccessful.

CHAPTER TWO

Rebuilding the Iraqi state

US war aims in Iraq were primarily about change: the removal of Saddam's regime and its replacement with one less prone to violent adventurism, domestic repression and the development of weapons of mass destruction. However, the almost complete collapse of the existing institutions of the state in the aftermath of victory gave rise to the more sustained problem of rebuilding all the structures of government throughout the country. The tasks facing the occupation have thus become more complex and potentially contradictory. Building a new political order will ultimately mean guiding Iraq towards a government that is in broad agreement with US foreign-policy aims. This will certainly involve minimising the role of former members of the old regime, and also identifying and marginalising other political forces that might destabilise a pro-US agenda. This has to be done in conjunction with the labour-intensive task of building a nationwide system of government. Finally, in recognition of regime change, the government has to be legitimate, both internationally and, more importantly, domestically. This will at some stage involve, not only giving the government back to suitable Iraqis, but back to an Iraqi governing élite either popularly elected, or which can at least repeatedly mobilise a significant section of Iraqi popular opinion in support of its rule.

Following the US military's seizure of Baghdad in April 2003, the sense of relief amongst the vast majority of the Iraqi population was clear; 35 years of tyranny had come to an end. By July 2003, this new space for political action had given rise to at least 140 different interest groups and political parties. In addition, 170 daily, weekly and monthly publications had sprung up, giving a platform to the diversity of views that could now be openly expressed.[1] This political mobilisation was fractured and diffuse, with no single group or party able to rally significant popular backing. However, as the CPA failed to deliver law and order or rejuvenate the infrastructure, a groundswell of support began to emerge for 'Iraqi ownership' of the state-building process. The US was faced with a dilemma: public opinion was demanding that it build government institutions that were stable, efficient and sustainable, but this was matched with increasing calls that Iraqis should manage this process. Which Iraqis should play this role, and how they should be chosen, was not at all clear.

The twin problems of building institutional capacity while at the same time promoting indigenous ownership is a tension at the heart of international attempts at state-building. Although international interventions into failed states have become increasingly common in the aftermath of the Cold War, the international community's record in delivering on the promise of intervention, building stable and democratic state structures before withdrawing, has proved to be poor. The task of recreating the institutions of a modern state in Iraq is as complex as in previous post-Cold War interventions. It is also proving to be highly costly in terms of time, human life and resources. The success of state-building is ultimately based on the quality and quantity of the governing institutions created in the aftermath of intervention. Crucially, this in turn is based on a state's ability to move from the deployment of despotic power to the deployment of infrastructural power. Despotic power is the application of military force, a governing élite's ability to impose its will on a population through the use of coercion.[2] This by its nature is an inefficient and ultimately unstable way to rule. The difficulties the US has had in simply attaining despotic power in Iraq are an indication of the magnitude of the task ahead.

For state-building to be successful, force has to be replaced by institutional rule. Power has to be centralised in a sovereign government, but that power has to be administrative, not military. The sovereign body at the head of a state generates directives for the wider governmental structures and laws for the population.[3] However, the efficiency of government is anchored in the ability of its apex to oversee the implementation of these directives throughout the whole of its administration. This can only be done through the creation of a regularised administrative staff, organised in a nationwide hierarchy of government offices. It is in this set of institutions that infrastructural power lies: 'the capacity of the state to penetrate civil society, and to implement logistically political decisions throughout the realm'.[4] Efficient administrative capacity is achieved and infrastructural power established once the population recognises the state as an essential and, most importantly, a legitimate presence in their everyday lives. Its regulation of society is then accepted as a necessity. This is the bureaucratic process that has to be enacted for regime change in Iraq to be successful, and for the US to leave behind a sustainable and legitimate state.

The legacy of Saddam Hussein

Iraqi regimes, because of their perceived domestic and international vulnerability, have with varying degrees of success sought to maximise their autonomy from society. This process has forced them to become dependent upon funding generated from outside Iraqi society. These resources were first supplied in the 1920s and 1930s by British government aid, and since 1958 they have come from oil revenue. Iraqi regimes have thus never had to rely on tax revenues, nor have they become beholden to domestic interest groups. This in turn gave governments increasing autonomy to control society. This process reached its apex under the Ba'athist regime built by Hasan al Bakr from 1968, and consolidated under Saddam after 1979. A powerful set of state institutions built up through the 1970s and 1980s reshaped Iraqi society, breaking organised resistance to Ba'athist rule and effectively atomising the population.

Although figures for oil revenue going to the Iraqi government remain disputed, it is safe to say that, after the oil shock of the early 1970s, vast sums of money began to flow into the government's treasury. Estimates put average annual oil revenue at $600 million from 1970 to 1972. By 1976, this figure had jumped to $8.5bn, and was up to $26bn by 1980. This had the effect of greatly increasing the Iraqi government's influence over society. For example, between 1958 and 1977 the number of personnel employed by the state jumped from 20,000 to 580,000. This figure does not include the estimated 230,000 people employed in the armed forces, or the 200,000 dependent on the state pension scheme. The total figure for the state payroll in 1990 was an estimated 822,000. These statistics point to the economic dominance that the state had built over society, with 21% of the active workforce and 40% of Iraqi households directly reliant on government payment.[5] Thus, changes in the political economy of Iraq in the 1970s delivered massive and unprecedented power to those who controlled the state. Due to land reform programmes instigated by the Ba'ath Party, the state became the largest landowner in Iraq.[6] The state also funnelled its new resources into a social-security system, new housing projects, and investments in health and education. By the 1970s,

Iraq's population was increasingly linked directly to the largesse of state institutions funded by oil wealth.

During the 1980s and 1990s, however, both the Iraqi state and its relations with society were transformed. The eight-year war with Iran, the 1990–91 Gulf War and finally the imposition of sanctions changed the Iraqi state, and with it Saddam's strategy of rule. From their application in 1990 until 1997, when UN-supervised oil revenues began to arrive, sanctions proved to be extremely efficient. They restricted the government's access to large-scale funding, which meant that economic policy was largely reactive, dominated by the short-term goal of staying in power. From 1991 until 2003 the effects of government policy and the sanctions regime led to hyperinflation, widespread poverty and malnutrition. The historically generous state welfare provision that had been central to the regime's governing strategy disappeared, and the government in Baghdad was forced to cut back on the resources it could devote to the armed forces and the police. Instead, Saddam concentrated his energies on keeping alive the informal networks of patronage and the security services that underpinned his rule, marginalising the Ba'ath Party as a vehicle for social mobilisation and control and relying on more informal and flexible methods of domination.[7] The large and well-educated middle class that formed the bedrock of Iraqi society became impoverished, and Iraq's once-complex and all-pervasive bureaucracy became hollowed out. Bribery was commonplace, as civil servants' official wages were almost valueless. State employees, teachers and medical staff had to manage as best they could, extracting resources from the impoverished people that depended on their services. Many professionals left public service, to take their chances in the private sector or flee into exile.

These were the institutions in which US planners had put their faith. To quote Condoleezza Rice, then the US National Security Advisor: 'The concept was that we would defeat the army, but the institutions would hold, everything from ministries to police forces'.[8] Through them, US forces planned to stabilise the country. Once order had been achieved, the occupiers would then move to reform and democratise the state. However, the state that the US had hoped to inherit was, by April 2003, on the verge of collapse following yet another war and three weeks of looting in its aftermath. Civil servants did not return to work after the ceasefire, instead opting to protect their families and property as best they could. Their offices across the country, but especially in Baghdad, were stripped by looters and burnt.[9] The combination of war, sanctions fatigue and rampant criminality led to complete state breakdown. In the aftermath of regime change, the Iraqi state had ceased to exist in any meaningful form. As a result, the subsequent extended exercise in state-building has been far more costly and has required much greater expertise and resources than the Pentagon anticipated. State institutions have to be painstakingly built from the ground up, and their relationship to society renegotiated. This has to be done in the face of increasing resentment, while meeting demands for Iraqi participation.

US planning before and after the war

The assumption that US forces would be able to utilise the functioning institutions of the Iraqi state was one of a series of miscalculations that undermined the coalition's approach to state-building. Many of these have their origins in a lack of preparation and sustained research into Iraq prior to the invasion. It has been speculated that influential neo-conservatives at the heart of Bush's administration, such as Deputy Secretary of Defense Paul Wolfowitz, spent their time in opposition during the late 1990s planning Saddam's removal from power. However, when they returned to government they appear to have devoted little time to substantive planning about what they would do with Iraq after Saddam was gone. The dominant assumptions about Iraq that shaped thinking, the nature of the experts consulted and the interaction between key governmental institutions all explain the flaws in pre-war planning.

The civilians in charge at the Pentagon had a long and close association with one of the exiled opposition parties, the Iraqi National Congress (INC), which was seen as the nucleus of a government-in-waiting. The INC's Ahmed Chalabi and his senior aides supplied the US government with information on Iraq's weapons of mass destruction programme, and on all other aspects of Iraqi government and society. The INC claimed that its information came from a widespread underground network of supporters in the country.[10] Chalabi himself was a key promoter of the 'decapitation' thesis. This argued that Saddam's government was extremely vulnerable and dependent on a small number of people. A strike aimed at the leadership would cause the government to collapse, leaving the institutions of the state in place. Those in charge at the Pentagon and White House accepted this assessment, along with excessively optimistic predictions about the welcome US troops would receive once they reached Iraq.[11] The need for major occupation forces or detailed planning was thus negated. High-level Iraqi participation in government would be provided by INC cadres.

The lack of substantive planning in the run-up to the war can also be explained by the internecine ideological battles that came to be a hallmark of the Bush presidency. As war became more likely, the State Department's Bureau of Near Eastern Affairs began to plan for the invasion's aftermath.

Under the stewardship of Thomas S. Warwick, who had spent a great deal of the 1990s studying Iraq for the US government, the 'Future of Iraq Project' assembled a broad array of Iraqi exiles in April 2002. The results provided a series of plans for dealing with the problems that might arise in post-war Iraq. By January 2003, the US government had centralised the planning process in the Pentagon after Bush signed a National Security Policy Directive authorising the coordination of Iraq policy. Given the antipathy, both personal and ideological, between the senior politicians running the Pentagon and the State Department, the work done by the Future of Iraq Project was disregarded in the run-up to and immediate aftermath of the invasion. Warwick and other senior Middle East experts at the State Department were actively discouraged from going to Baghdad.[12]

The civilian responsibility for post-war Iraq was assigned to the Office of Reconstruction and Humanitarian Assistance (ORHA), run by a retired general, Jay Garner, under the authority of the Pentagon. Prior to the invasion, planning focused on developing a capacity for disaster management, the ability to cope with mass movements of displaced people, widespread food shortages and the consequences of WMD use, none of which happened. Ultimately, the civil arm of the invasion did not have the capacity to play the role required of it in the aftermath of war, a shadow state, running the essential services of government. ORHA was equally constrained by the military's rules of engagement, which did not let its staff move about Baghdad without military escorts.

The legacies of the Pentagon's pre-war approach to Iraqi planning continued to dog the occupation after ORHA was dissolved into the new body running Iraq, the Coalition Provisional Authority, and after Bremer had replaced Garner in May 2003. As with pre-war planning, one of the main problems hampering the occupation was the acute lack of knowledge about the country. The occupation authorities took up residence in the old seat of government, the Republican Palace at the heart of the secure 'green zone' in the centre of Baghdad. However, with almost no expertise of its own the CPA became dependent upon the same small group of Iraqi exiles that had advised it about Iraq's politics and WMD before the invasion. This core group was meant to act as a conduit between US forces and the Iraqi population. Despite being absent from the country for many years, its members were supposed to advise the American administrators struggling to rebuild the country. Finally, and most importantly, it was hoped that they would become the basis of the new political élite and form the core of Iraq's new governing classes. However, the Iraqi parties allied to the INC, dominated by the KDP and the PUK, brought with them a distinctive view of Iraqi society. They argued that Iraq was irrevocably divided between sectarian and religious groupings, mobilised by deep communal antipathy. This 'primordialisation' of Iraq clearly influenced the way the first governing council was formed, in July 2003, but it bore little resemblance to the real state of Iraqi society in 2003–2004.[13]

The heavy reliance on organisations like Allawi's Iraqi National Accord (INA) and the INC widened the divide between Iraqi society and US forces. Despite setting up numerous offices around Baghdad, publishing party newspapers and spending liberally, the two main exile groups found it difficult to rally any popular support. A series of interviews carried out by the author with a cross-section of Iraqis in Baghdad in May 2003 – rich and poor, religious and secular – revealed at best indifference and, more usually, anger towards the returned exiles, especially the avowedly secular INC and INA.[14] Those interviewed included one Baghdadi who, under Saddam's rule, had worked secretly for one of the exiled groups. He was arrested and sentenced to death, a fate he only avoided after nine months in the notorious Abu Ghraib prison because of the regime's pre-invasion amnesty. When asked about the party for which he nearly lost his life, he replied: 'I would have done anything to see the back of Saddam. But since the exiles have returned I have been disappointed, I do not trust them'.[15] Off the record, candid former exiles admitted that they had been surprised by the difficulties they faced after returning. Instead of being welcomed, they found a sullen and suspicious population that has largely refused to offer its political loyalty to the newly returned parties.

The lack of communication between American civil servants and military personnel and the population of Iraq was the main factor which undermined the occupation. From an inability to interact with Iraqi society sprang the core problems facing the US. Intelligence gathering was difficult because Iraqis felt alienated from both the CPA and the returned exiles. It would be a brave Iraqi who would have risked her or his life by giving information to a transient organisation apparently so detached from the everyday concerns of the population.

Building political structures in post-Saddam Iraq
Against a background of state collapse, increased violence and insecurity, plans for rebuilding the political and administrative structures in Iraq went through a series of distinct phases. As the size and nature of the task began to dawn on the CPA, administrators faced a series of potentially competing needs. The role of former Ba'athists in the government had to be minimised. This was deemed necessary not only to pursue the ultimate

goal of regime change, but also to create a space within which a new ruling élite could be nurtured. However, this policy objective clashed with the demands of the Iraqi population for the speedy restoration of order and government services. The political decision to pursue de-Ba'athification and expel many former administrators from the civil service delayed the technocratic goal of restoring services. Finally, the CPA faced a highly mobilised society vocally expressing its newfound political freedom. Against this background, the CPA was committed to the management of political transition and élite participation in governing structures. This had to be balanced with a commitment to democracy and the need for the nascent political structures to be seen as both Iraqi and legitimate. As policy changed to meet each of these pressing and potentially contradictory factors, little attention was paid to the consequences of each new initiative.

Garner's approach to state-building and self-government appears to have been influenced by his close relationship with both the formerly exiled parties influential in pre-invasion Washington and the main Kurdish parties, the KDP and PUK. His inclinations were to meet the legitimacy deficit head-on, and place as much responsibility in the hands of these Iraqis as quickly as possible. He would manage the transition by promoting Iraqi politicians familiar to the US.[16] To this end, two meetings were held in March and April 2003 to form a body which would act as a forum for Iraqi political opinion. These meetings were designed to draw Iraqis together into some form of representative assembly. The first meeting, at Ur near Nasiriyah on 15 March, was dominated by Iraqis recently returned from exile. Its legitimacy was challenged by a large demonstration outside, which highlighted the small number of delegates (80) and the dubious nature of their claims to be representative of anything more than themselves. Although the turnout in the second meeting, in Baghdad on 28 April, was larger at 300, it did not reach the 2,000–3,000 predicted.[17] The fact that over half the attendees were exiles pointed to a larger problem of confidence in the US occupation and the dangers of alignment with it. The process was plagued by an awareness of the rising unpopularity of the US presence; believing it to be temporary, Iraqis chose to eschew involvement in political and administrative institutions until the situation had become clearer and the risks of political involvement fewer.

One of Bremer's first decisions on arriving in Baghdad in May 2003 was to delay moves towards delegating responsibility to a leadership council largely composed of the exiled parties. This was in recognition that the building of a credible government was going to take a great deal longer than had been anticipated. Bremer's approach was to bring managerial coherence to the organisation of the occupation, while slowing down the delegation of power to Iraqis until it was clear which group or groups could win the support of a significant proportion of the population.

This careful, incremental but largely undemocratic approach was set aside with the arrival of the United Nations Special Representative for Iraq, Vieira de Mello. As an international diplomat with many years' experience, the primary issue in Iraq for Vieira de Mello was not the security vacuum or the pressing need to increase governmental efficiency, but the lack of a sovereign body that could represent the aspirations of ordinary Iraqis. To that end, he persuaded Bremer that a governing body of Iraqis should be set up to act as a repository of Iraqi sovereignty.[18]

The CPA, in conjunction with the United Nations, set up the Iraqi Governing Council (IGC) in July 2003. The IGC's membership was chosen by Bremer after extended negotiations between the CPA, Vieira de Mello and the seven dominant, formerly exiled parties. The CPA promoted the IGC as 'the most representative body in Iraq's history'. The representative nature of the IGC could not, however, come from the undemocratic method of its formation. Instead, the CPA focused on the supposedly 'balanced' nature of its membership. The politicians it had chosen were believed to represent the ethnic and religious make-up of Iraq: 13 Shias, five Sunnis, five Kurds, a Turkomen and a Christian. The forced and rather bizarre nature of this arrangement was highlighted by the inclusion of Hamid Majid Mousa, the Iraqi Communist Party's representative, and the then avowedly secular Chalabi himself in the 'Shia bloc' of 13. Such sectarian mathematics were also used to expand the number of cabinet portfolios to 25, so that offices (and, more importantly, the resources that came with them) could be divided up in a similar fashion. The manner of the IGC's selection caused a great deal of consternation across Iraqi opinion. Criticism focused on the divisive nature of the selection process, arguing that it had introduced an overt sectarianism that had previously not been central to Iraqi political discourse.[19] Debate also centred on the possible damage such a selection process would do to government efficiency, with complaints that council members should have been chosen for their technical skills, rather than their party, sectarian or religious affiliations.

The council's inaugural meeting was held in July, but by early November Bremer and senior US officials in the CPA had already become disillusioned with its inability to deliver either strategic leadership or legitimacy. In a series of coordinated leaks and off-the-record briefings to the press, the council was described by US administrators as a central part of the problem then undermining the occupation. Bremer noted that 'at least half the council is out of the country at any given time and that at some meetings, only four or five members show up'. Senior American CPA officials argued that 'the council has been seriously remiss in oversight of its own ministers' and most seriously had been 'inept at outreach to its own people'.[20] For those in the CPA trying to stem the rising tide of violence sweeping Iraq in the winter of 2003, a new approach was needed; as a senior occupation official said at the time, 'it is unlikely that we will want to make a provisional government out of a council that has been feckless'.[21]

Negative international press coverage of the shortcomings of the IGC combined with the rising numbers of casualties among coalition forces resulted in Bremer's hasty recall to Washington for consultations. Faced with growing pressure from the UN Security Council for real sovereign power to be delegated to an Iraqi governing body, the increasing alienation of the Iraqi population from the CPA and a rising tide of political violence, Bremer's cautious and incremental approach was abandoned. The Bush administration set 30 June 2004 as the deadline for transferring sovereignty to Iraq. The US plan was endorsed by the IGC on 15 November 2003. It envisaged the drafting of a 'fundamental law' by the end of February 2004, to be followed by the creation of a transitional assembly of between 200 and 500 delegates. This assembly was to select a cabinet and a leader for Iraq, and guide the country to democratic elections, scheduled for the spring of 2005. Although hopes for 'Iraqi ownership' of this truncated process rested with the transitional assembly, it was not to be directly elected. Instead, a series of indirect elections and caucuses was to be held.

This complex process drew immediate criticism from several sectors of Iraq's newly emergent civil society. Most importantly, the senior Shia cleric Marja Ayatollah Ali al-Sistani publicly set himself against the 'caucusing' approach, restating his long-held position that a constitutional assembly should be elected by universal suffrage. In January 2004, 100,000 people demonstrated in Baghdad in an effort to convince the CPA that Sistani's objections could not be ignored. With the apparently intransigent opposition of Sistani, the US government came face to face with the contradictions inherent in its position. With increasing Iraqi opposition to the occupation, the CPA had to delegate real power to Iraqis. However, for both administrative and political reasons, the CPA felt that it was not possible to hold nationwide elections to choose that new sovereign body.

Faced with the seemingly irreconcilable demands of powerful local actors and the forthcoming US presidential elections, the White House turned to the United Nations, and Lakhdar Brahimi. Brahimi, fresh from his mission to stabilise Afghanistan and already well acquainted with key Iraqi players, appeared to be the only mediator who could move the process forward. Starting with a fact-finding trip in February 2004 and two subsequent missions, Brahimi's team consulted widely across Iraq's population, gathering views on the nature of the problems facing any new government, as well as possible solutions. The resulting plan was designed not only to tide Iraq over from 30 June until the earliest possible date for elections, in January 2005, but also to dissipate the tensions between managing the transition to a new government and building administrative capacity to establish legitimacy. It accepted Sistani's demands that only a democratically elected government should be given sustained political power by opting for an interim administration with a clearly defined time limit and restricted authority. It also acknowledged the results of opinion polls, which indicated widespread mistrust of the politicians involved in the IGC, and a popular desire to be ruled by people appointed for their skills and qualifications.[22]

Brahimi proposed a new caretaker government comprising technocrats chosen for their experience rather than their party-political allegiances. This administration would manage the government during the interregnum before elections. Crucially, he called on those appointed to disavow party politics. This would have guaranteed that the powers of the nascent state were not used to benefit any of the parties competing for power. In creating a technocratic élite committed to government service rather than politics, the Brahimi plan could have established the basis of an apolitical civil service. Finally, by excluding political parties from government, Brahimi was forcing them out of the 'green zone' and into the country. The parties that dominated the IGC had not even started to create national party networks that could mobilise popular support and deliver it to the ballot box. By demanding that these parties switch their energies from government to society, Brahimi was hoping that they would act as channels for public opinion, linking the polity to its government.

The third pillar of the Brahimi plan was the convening of a national conference, consisting of 1,000–1,500 delegates. Its role would be to oversee the interim government, scrutinising its legislation. It would also start the process of national dialogue, instituting consultative channels between society and the state. Crucially, it would provide a venue within which those opposed to the US occupation could make their views known, integrating the more radical and alienated voices into the political process before elections.[23]

The American authorities' treatment of Brahimi on his third and final trip to Baghdad in May 2004 indicated the limits of any future role for the United Nations, and the self-imposed restrictions on America's intervention in the Iraqi polity. Brahimi's influence over personalities and events was not based on Security Council resolutions or the institutional commitment of the UN to a sustained role. Instead, Brahimi's position rested on personal assurances he had been given from the highest levels in Washington. The logic of his approach was underpinned by an assumption that US political weight would be brought to bear to impose his plan. The core of his approach, the disbanding of the IGC and its members' ejection into Iraqi society to vie for election, was likely to be unpopular with the political parties dominating the Governing Council. But Brahimi's assumption that the CPA would be willing to forcibly intervene in the political process and face the animosity of the IGC proved to be wrong.

Brahimi's third trip to Baghdad came at the end of the worst period of violence faced by the coalition. US forces were fighting revolts on two fronts, one centred on the siege of Falluja and the other driven by Sadr. Brahimi's arrival was also greeted with an upsurge of negative coverage in the Baghdad press, which was dominated by the parties of the Governing Council.[24] Relations between the IGC and Brahimi were described by one Council member as 'war'.[25] Against this background, Brahimi did not get the help he was expecting from the CPA, or indeed from Washington. Involved in increasingly acrimonious negotiations and with little support, Brahimi raised the prospect of his resignation, but in the end retreated and let the Governing Council and the CPA dictate the terms of the new interim government.[26]

This government was the very antithesis of the Brahimi plan. Far from being dominated by technocrats who had disavowed any involvement in politics, the Interim Iraqi Government was full of party placemen. The most senior figure, Allawi, was the leader of Iraqi National Accord. The vice-president, Ibrahim Jaafari, was the head of the Dawa Party, one of the two main Shia parties. The other vice-president, Rowsch Shaways, was a senior member of the KDP. Ministerial posts were divided among the other parties that dominated the old IGC. It appears that, faced with threats of instability and possible violence, the CPA chose to co-opt key members of the Governing Council rather than try to find an alternative, indigenous basis for a new administrative and ruling élite. After describing IGC members as 'feckless' and incapable of reaching out to the wider Iraqi population the previous November, the CPA brought these same people back into government. By implication it entrusted them and their parties with the creation of Iraq's new state, and oversight of its evolving democracy. The initial decision to invest in the individuals and party organisations who attained prominence in exile has come to dominate the whole approach to reconstituting government. This has the benefit of allowing a managed transition from the Ba'athist regime to a new governing élite. However, the administrative capacity of this new élite is unproven. Its ability to work efficiently and harmoniously with the remnants of the old civil service, the police and the army is open to question. Finally, and most importantly, its ability to build a base within Iraqi society, to mobilise a significant portion of public opinion and bring legitimacy to the new government, is highly questionable.

The Elections of 2005

The Transitional Administrative Law agreed in March 2004 set a clear time-table for progress towards democracy, stating that national elections must be held no later than the end of January 2005. These polls selected a 275-member assembly, which is scheduled to serve for a year. During that time, it will ratify the choice of a president and two deputies, who will in turn choose one of the assembly's members to serve as prime minister. The assembly's main task, however, is to draft a constitution by the middle of August 2005. This constitution will be submitted to a referendum no later than October 2005, and then used to conduct elections for a fully constitutional government by 15 December. This government will take power by the end of 2005.

The countdown to the elections started on 1 November 2004, with voter registration. The electoral roll was based on existing information collected for the ration distribution system. An audit of this data indicates that it was up to 83% accurate.[27] From the beginning of November 2004, the heads of all households in Iraq were asked to confirm the names of those in their families old enough to vote. If the rationing information proved to be incorrect, they were directed to one of the 545 electoral registration centres across the county to update the register of voters. The Independent Electoral Commission of Iraq employed 6,000 local staff to run the registration centres, and managed to open all but 90 of them.[28]

The next stage in the process was the registration of the candidates and parties seeking election. The Transitional Administrative Law set stringent standards of eligibility. Candidates had to have a 'good reputation', have no criminal convictions 'involving moral turpitude' and must not have been senior members of the Ba'ath Party or the old regime's secret services. Candidates had to sign a declaration certifying that they met these terms, and collect 500 signatures in support of their application.[29] By the election, a total of 7,785 candidates had registered to take part, loosely organised in 111 parties and coalitions.[30]

The election itself was structured around a single constituency, with all voters voting for all candidates. On the day, a candidate needed to obtain more than 30,750 votes in order to secure a seat in parliament.[31] In addition to organising the election around one national constituency, the candidates and parties seeking election were encouraged to run as part of a nation-wide list, with those at the top standing the best chance of being elected. The chief of the UN's Electoral Assistance Division, Carina Perelli, argued that the choice of a single constituency for the whole country and the use of a list system had two potential advantages. First, in a country without a state, and with a security vacuum, this approach would keep the need for electoral institutions to a minimum, reducing targets for the insurgents, while limiting the need for a complex bureaucracy. Second, it overtly aimed to shape the election. By having one large constituency and encouraging lists to compete in that constituency, the hope was that different parties would form coalitions to stand a better chance of maximising their votes, in the process uniting Iraq's communities within each coalition.

Reports early on in the electoral process indicated that the US embassy in Baghdad favoured what was termed a 'monster coalition' list. The aim was to unite all the parties that had dominated the Iraqi Governing Council, and which formed the bulk of the interim government's cabinet. The plan was promoted on the basis that it would prevent any one party or group from dominating the administration, allowing Iraq's first elected government to rule in a pluralistic and consensual manner.[32] The plan was widely attacked as being anti-democratic, not giving the electorate a choice of parties to vote for and yet again suppressing the growth of indigenous political parties by favouring those that had recently returned from exile.[33]

The US embassy's hopes that a coalition ticket would dominate the elections were ended by the overt intervention of Sistani. In mid-October, his spokesperson announced that the Ayatollah had encouraged the formation of a six-person committee, led by Hussein Shahristani, a former nuclear scientist jailed by Saddam for 12 years, to 'coordinate' the creation of a 'Shia' list for the elections. Parties and individuals could join this list if they agreed to vote as a bloc in the new parliament, not to challenge the 'Islamic character' of the Iraqi people and not to back any legislation that ran counter to Sharia law.[34] Early negotiations focused on the proportion of political parties versus independent candidates to be placed on the list, and whether Sadr could be persuaded to join. However, indications are that, out of a total of 228 candidates put forward by the list, less than half represented the 11 parties in the coalition, and less then six were from the Shia religious establishment. The rest were individuals picked by committee to represent a wider sample of Iraqi society.[35]

As the election campaign began in earnest, it became clear that only two other coalitions had the ability to mount a serious challenge to the United

Iraqi Alliance organised by Shahristani and blessed by Sistani. The first was the Iraqi List of the temporary prime minister, Ayad Allawi. Allawi deployed a large campaign budget (reputed to be as much as £2.14m) and slick advertising to dominate terrestrial and satellite television. Focusing on a secular and security agenda, he presented himself as a strong leader, appealing to the middle class as the only person capable of restoring order.[36] The second was a united list formed by the KDP and PUK in an attempt to maximise the Kurdish vote and Kurdish influence over the drafting of the new constitution.

The election itself was dominated by different styles of campaigning. The Shia list, as it quickly became known, stressed its religious credentials and the tacit backing of Sistani. In the last few days of the campaign, once it was assured of a majority, those directing campaigning belatedly became aware of the dangers of fighting the election on such a potentially sectarian platform, and began to use more secular imagery and cross-communal appeals. The Shia list shied away from calling for US troops to leave Iraq in the aftermath of elections, realising that it did not have to indulge in such popularism to assure its victory, and aware that, as the core of the next government, it would be heavily dependent on US forces for its survival.[37] A worrying development was the use for electioneering of the police and National Guard units by both the Shia list in the south and Allawi's coalition in and around Baghdad. The blatant politicisation of the nascent security services so early on in the life of the new state does not bode well for its future stability.[38]

In the event, on election day on 30 January, eight and a half million Iraqis voted in the first democratic elections of their lives. Despite as many as nine suicide bombings in Baghdad, and insurgent attacks across the country rising from the usual daily total of 60–70 to 260, 58% of those eligible to vote did so. Electoral turn-out varied dramatically across the country and across Iraq's different ethnic and religious communities. In the northern areas dominated by the Kurdish population, turnout was between 82% and 92%. In the southern districts, where the majority of the population is Shia, between 61% and 71% turned out. The Shia list, the United Iraqi Alliance, won 48% of the vote and 146 seats in the 275-member assembly. The Kurdish Alliance won 77 seats, and Allawi's list won 13% of the vote and 40 seats.[39]

The boycott demanded by the political organisations representing the Sunni population appeared to have been successful, with only 2% voting in Anbar province, an area of north-western Iraq with a high concentration of Sunni voters. The boycott means that the Sunni community, as much as a quarter of the whole population, will not be represented in the new assembly. A coalition of Sunni mosques across the country, the Association of Muslim

Scholars (*Hayat al-Ulama al-Muslimin*), led the campaign to boycott the elections. After the US assault on Falluja it was joined by the Iraqi Islamic Party, whose leader, Mohsen Abdul Hamid, called for the elections to be postponed for six months. By mid-November 2004, the Association of Muslim Scholars had been joined by 14 other organisations to form the Iraqi Founding National Assembly, an umbrella group for all those refusing to take part in the polls while the country remained occupied by US forces. This group may well evolve into a broad anti-occupation front, acting as the political voice for the various different groups involved in the insurgency.

Indications of future problems: the interim constitution

The newly elected assembly now has the task of drafting the new constitution and electing a three-person presidential council, which in turn will choose the new prime minister. Ibrahim al Jaafari, head of the Shia Dawa Party, is expected to become prime minister. He will have the majority of executive power, pick the cabinet and run Iraq until the next set of elections held under the new constitution, at present scheduled for 15 December 2005.

The drafting of the Transitional Administrative Law, which was finally agreed on 2 March 2004, gives a strong indication of the debates and schisms that may well come to dominate the new assembly. The law was a temporary document aimed largely at guiding the interim government through to the next elections at the end of 2005. Despite its temporary role and aspirational language, the Transitional Administrative Law was the focus of intense political debate and acrimony. The two most controversial issues in its drafting, and the issues set to dominate the new assembly, are the role that Islam and the Kurds are to play in the new state.

The interim constitution's importance lies in the path it charts for the evolution of Iraq's democracy. It also highlights the main fault-lines that will shape the polity over the next decade. The two main Kurdish parties, the PUK and the KDP, have effectively run two independent fiefdoms in the north of Iraq since 1991. How, and indeed if, these two areas are to be reintegrated into Iraq is one of the most difficult issues the country will have to face over the coming years. Both the KDP and PUK have independent and well-armed militias which gave them leverage in the negotiating process. US officials had to persuade both to postpone their central demand that they be given a fixed percentage of oil revenue and be allowed to increase the geographical area over which they rule. In the end, a compromise was reached whereby the interim constitution recognised that Iraq will not only be democratic, but also federal. This would allow for the devolution of power to the regions. But negotiations circumvented arguments about what type of federal system will be used, or the degree of autonomy the two Kurdish organisations will be allowed to retain. A decision on these substantive issues was postponed until the end of the transitional period in 2005.

The issue of religion will also be important in shaping how Iraq develops in the coming years. The liberal ambitions of some IGC members resulted in a commitment to protect the freedom of worship of all Iraq's citizens. However, arguments about the role that Islam will play in the political and legislative life of the country were hard-fought. The debate centred on whether Islam should be *the* or only *a* main source for future legislation. In January 2004, the Council appeared to indicate its preference by voting to allow Islamic law to override civil law in matters of divorce and inheritance. In the end, Bremer intervened in the debate surrounding religion, refusing to recognise the January decision and forcing a compromise in the wording of the constitution.

The Transitional Administrative Law was an idealistic document representative of the aspirations of its drafters, rather than the practical possibilities of its imposition. That such a document could cause such political conflict within the IGC indicates what will be involved in the political debates surrounding the drawing up of the new constitution during 2005.

Conclusions

The interim government led by Allawi was granted international legal sovereignty by the UN Security Council on 8 June 2004. The election of a new government in January 2005 effectively ends its short and turbulent tenure. The main task facing the government that takes over from Allawi is to establish some form of domestic sovereignty to match the international sovereignty given back to Iraq in 2004. Unlike international sovereignty, domestic sovereignty, 'the organisation and effectiveness of political authority', is based on the quality and depth of the relationship between the governed and the governing.[40] This relationship is clearly about institutional capacity, but it is also about legitimacy. Governments must not only be seen to be ruling, but their actions must be felt to be in the interests of the people. For the government elected in 2005 to be successful, it will have to make substantive progress in engendering a degree of legitimacy. It will have to convince a sizeable proportion of the Iraqi population that it is ruling in their interests, furthering their collective ideas of what Iraq is and what it is to become.

For the Iraqi people, traumatised by a brutal dictatorship, war and months of lawlessness and violence, the legitimate expression of political opinion only began on 9 April 2003. Most of the political parties now being used as the cornerstone of the interim government were imported into the country after the regime fell. Thus, they have had only a relatively short period of time to gain the attention of the population, much less win their trust or allegiance. Baghdad is certainly awash with political parties, its streets decorated with a wide variety of slogans and its pavements covered with discarded copies of dozens of party newspapers. There is little evidence, however, that this political ferment has solidified into nation-wide institutionalised party politics, or that the numerous organisations attempting to court the loyalty of Iraqis have been successful.

No indigenous civil society organisations survived Saddam's rule. The population was largely atomised by 35 years of Ba'athist dictator-ship. Liberation has certainly led to political mobilisation, but this proc-ess is tentative, unstable and highly fractured.No one individual or party has managed to rally significant support from the population. Iraq at the time of the elections was a country still lacking effective institutions, mili-tary, administrative or political. The two political parties at the core of the victorious United Iraqi Alliance, the Dawa Party and the Supreme Council for the Islamic Revolution in Iraq, were swept to power not by their own organisation, canvassing or legitimacy but by their association with Sist-ani. The danger is that they will not solidify the mass societal mobilisation of the election by building mass party organisations.

Since its creation in 1920, Iraq has never had a stable functioning democ-racy. The legacies that Saddam has left the country will make building a sustainable democracy extremely difficult. The Ba'ath Party co-opted or broke the civil and political organisations it could not control. People were encouraged through violence and patronage to interact with the institutions of the state on a personal basis. Attempting to build organised, institutional-ised party politics in Iraq is possible, but it will take both time and effort. The grave danger for the Iraqi polity, the region and the wider world is that those who run the state will feel that they have neither the time nor the support to take this route. Those who have been elected to run the state, the representa-tives of the nascent political parties that dominate the victorious United Iraqi Alliance, are competing among themselves and with the other coalitions that fought the elections for the allegiance of the Iraqi people. Instead of going on to build a liberal democracy, they may adopt another model popular in the region and across the developing world: neo-patrimonialism. This would deploy state resources to buy political loyalty. The Iraqi population would then come to experience politics not as citizens interacting with a neutral, legal and rational state to which they could give their collective loyalty, but as subjects whose quiescence is bought through state resources, and whose votes and political participation are meaningless.

CHAPTER THREE

Political mobilisation in the new Iraq

Beyond the collapsed governmental institutions of the Iraqi state, a potentially even larger problem, that of Iraqi society, now faces the new Iraqi government and its American advisers. How that society, traumatised by war, sanctions and dictatorship, begins to mobilise to make its opinions felt will be crucial to how the country, and the region beyond it, evolves. After 35 years of autocracy, politics in Iraq are highly fluid, and societal certainties are few and far between. How the new state is built will be the key factor influencing societal mobilisation. The way the institutions of the new state make their presence felt in the everyday lives of ordinary Iraqis, will play a major role in shaping the state, the degree to which the population gives their loyalty, and are prepared to defend it.

Emerging trends within Iraqi society are important factors in this equation. As the state slowly increases its influence, it will have to seek out intermediaries within civil society, both individuals and groups, to act as conduits for information and resources. This process will empower these organisations, as they become key figures in state–society relations, the recipients of state resources but also the sources of governmental information about society. The choice of which organisations within society are useful conduits will depend on how civil servants and politicians running the bureaucracy understand Iraqi society, which groups they perceive to be influential or useful, and which groups they see as a hindrance to state-building and the creation of order. These choices will influence not only the evolution of state–society relations, but society itself. If those running the Iraqi state get these decisions wrong, in the sense of favouring individuals and groups without a sustainable base within the population, this will add to instability and undermine the foundations of the state.[1]

Empirical information about Iraqi society is extremely limited: the UN, for example, laments the 'dearth of demographic information about Iraq's population over the past several decades'.[2] During the 1970s and 1980s, the Ba'athist regime was reluctant to release any data concerning the population or the economy. This changed during the 1990s, when the government published statistical information to support its battle against sanctions. This information, which included the 1997 census, was of inferior quality and tainted by a strong suspicion that the figures had been manipulated.

International estimates put the population in 2003 at 25.9m people, rising to 27.1m in 2004. Of these, 40% were under 14 years of age. Close to 70% of people live in urban areas.[3] However, the statistics that cause the most controversy are those seeking to describe the ethnic and religious make-up of the country. Throughout Iraq's history, all statistical information relating to these issues has tended to be based on approximations. The British, in the 18 years that they controlled the country (1914–32), never carried out a census. At independence in 1932, 53% of the population were thought to be Arab Shia Muslims, 21% Arab Sunnis and 14% Sunni Kurds. The rest (12%) were Arab Christians, Turkomen and Jews.[4] Today, the US Central Intelligence Agency puts the Arab population at 75–80% and the Kurds at 15–20%. The Shia Arabs comprise 60–65% and the Sunnis, including the majority of the Kurds, 32–37%.[5]

With the empirical data on Iraq of such questionable reliability, and given the former regime's control on access to the country, those writing on and analysing the population have been forced to replace hard data with conjecture and theoretical speculation. One of the most common responses to this empirical lacuna is a primordial reading of Iraq's society. This argument tends to have three themes. The starting-point is the supposedly deeply divided nature of Iraqi society. For this school of thought, personified in the writing of Leslie Gelb and Peter Galbraith, Iraq has 'three distinct and sectarian communities', Sunni, Shia and Kurd.[6] These communities, it is argued, are largely geographically homogenous, deeply divided and mutually hostile. Having been locked in an artificial, Sunni-dominated state for 84 years, these three groups have descended into internecine hostility. This analysis leads its protagonists to one conclusion: the division of Iraq into three smaller, ethnically purer and more manageable states.

Academic experts studying the social and political evolution of the country as a whole, as opposed to the Kurdish region in isolation, have long stressed that the description of Iraq as a society divided into three mutually hostile communities is a static caricature that does great damage to a complex historical reality. Comparative academic examinations of ethnic identities around the world stress that they are fluid and often historically discontinuous.[7] They are formed by and react to the changing nature of society, and how a state seeks to interact with and control its population. With this in mind it is clear that Iraqis, like all of us, have several different aspects to their political and societal identities: familial, professional, geographic, as well as ethnic and religious. These are not static but change over time, and react to the politics of any given moment. A political situation and its history will determine which social identity will be most important to the individuals involved. On occasions, ethnic or religiously based identities may come to dominate political mobilisation, but equally, political action could be based on the position of the individual within wider society, their job or their education. Crucial to the choices made are the institutional capacity of those groups and organisations seeking to mobilise support, and the ideological resources they have to work with: essentially, how individuals perceive themselves and their communities. To continually select one aspect of an individual's identity above all others, in this case ethnic and religious identity, or to pick a specific moment of Iraqi history, 'a golden age', as definitive, is certainly overly deterministic, even racist. An analytical judgement of how Iraq's population will seek to mobilise in the future will certainly have to study its religious and ethnic divisions. But it has to do this with a historical perspective, seeking to identify the sources of political identity and trends that run counter to religion and ethnicity, or that support them.

In the case of Iraq, Saddam's regime was dominated by one group of politicians, the majority of whom were Arab Sunni Muslims. However, the governing élite rested on 'the narrowest power base in Iraq's history'.[8] The ruling élite was not the product of the Sunni community as a whole, but the extended family of one man, Saddam Hussein, and his Tikrit-based clan. This organisation of power did not simply represent the interests or aspirations of the wider Sunni community in Iraq. Saddam's ruling strategy deliberately excluded Sunnis who were not from Tikrit, and Tikritis who were not from the three families at the heart of the ruling group.[9] Those living in and around the north-west of Iraq suffered greatly under Saddam because they were geographically and administratively close to the ruling élite and the greatest immediate threat. Ba'athist rule originally based on Iraqi and Arab nationalism mutated during the 1980s into a cult of personality focused on Saddam and designed to enrich his immediate family. This was not a 'Sunni-dominated' state: by the 1990s it was a state ultimately ruled by and for Saddam's family.

Under Saddam's guidance, the state set about using its power and wealth to transform society. Throughout the late 1970s and 1980s individual Iraqis became increasingly aware that their new-found economic prosperity was dependent upon their loyalty to a regime dominated by Saddam. As political dissidents across Iraqi society discovered, particularly in areas of the north and south with Kurdish and Shia majorities, questioning government authority or campaigning for change had political and economic consequences. Politically, the new wealth of the state was largely spent on the army and the security services: 40% of oil wealth during this period went on arms purchases that directly increased the state's ability to control the population. The state used its resources to bind individuals and sections of society to it on the basis of loyalty to Saddam and his ruling élite. Dissent, perceived or real, would be punished economically in the first instance and, if more serious, with the deployment of the state's vastly increased capacity for organised violence.

By the late 1980s, Iraqi society had been effectively atomised, with intermediate institutions, political, economic or social, broken by the military and economic power of the regime. Those societal institutions the regime thought useful were reconstituted under government patronage to serve as vehicles for mobilisation, resource distribution and control.[10] Trade unions and social organisations external to the state were either co-opted or dismantled. Individuals found their welfare and economic needs depended upon their own unmediated relations with the state.[11] Put simply, there was no functioning civil society in Iraq before regime change in 2003.[12] The Ba'athist regime's attack on civil society meant that personal ties to family and extended family, town, city or neighbourhood, as well as to province and religion, were the only ties to survive, though in a diffuse and disorganised way.[13]

At the same time, the regime invested energy in attempting to build a version of Iraqi nationalism that would suit its needs. During the Iran–Iraq war in the 1980s it struggled to construct a single national discourse that could rally all communities to the nation's defence. Diverse cultural symbols from Iraq's pre-Islamic past and current history were mixed with Shia and Kurdish themes.[14] This produced results: 80% of the rank and file and 20% of the officer corps of the old Iraqi army were Shias, yet they fought loyally for Iraq throughout the gruelling eight-year war with Iran, a state with a Shia majority.[15] Explanations of this phenomenon cannot simply concentrate on ethnic identity, but must instead acknowledge the strength of Iraqi nationalism. This became especially influential after the Iranian army made inroads into Iraqi territory after 1983.

After the ceasefire with Iran in 1988 and the increasing economic hardship that the population faced, analysts detected a split between the popular nationalism of the public and the officially promoted instrumental chauvinism of the Ba'athist government. This divergence reached its peak in 1991 with the rebellions in the aftermath of the ceasefire that marked the end of the second Gulf War.[16] However, the trauma of war and a rapid decline in living standards and social structures led to the strengthening of a militant Iraqi nationalism. The state-inspired credo of Arab nationalism has historically found support among a population that thinks that Iraq was unjustly treated by the West and the international system. The 12 years of suffering under sanctions fuelled the rise of a powerful nationalism, born of a stubborn pride that Iraq had managed to survive despite everything that had occurred. The present situation cannot but exacerbate such perceptions. The failure of Baghdad's liberated population to offer the ecstatic welcome to US troops predicted in Washington is indicative of the power of nationalism in Iraq.

Across the south and centre of Iraq, organised political mobilisation has had to start from scratch since April 2003. Two trends are detectable in the resultant movements, for both the Shia and Sunni sections of society. In the first place, a strong unitary state with Baghdad as its capital has become a key aspiration, underpinned by a strong Iraqi nationalism. But, at the same time, opinion has remained fluid, with no one group or coherent manifesto rallying a majority of the population. The tensions that have emerged between the Kurdish parties in the north on the one hand and the Shia political parties and religious establishment on the other are indicative of a wider division. Although all major political parties across Iraq are committed to the territorial integrity of the country, their visions of what that country should evolve into are distinctly different, and possibly at odds.

Trends within the Shia community

As a majority of the population, the political aspirations of Iraq's Shia will be a defining factor in how post-Saddam Iraq evolves. This process will unfold mainly in the cities most holy to Shia Islam, Najaf and Karbala, and across the south of the country. But it will also make itself felt in Baghdad, in al Tharwa (renamed Sadr City), a township of two million people built in the early 1960s in the east of the capital.

Shia political opinion has been shaped by three competing groups: the religious hierarchy based in Najaf and Karbala, the urban middle-class intellectuals, and a once-thriving entrepreneurial and mercantile class.[17] Since 1920, these disparate groups have come to agree on the broad principles around which they have rallied public opinion. At the heart of this approach sits a strong commitment to Iraqi nationalism and a unified Iraqi state. The Shia religious hierarchy, or *ulama*, mobilised rural Iraqis against British occupation in the name of a nascent Iraqi nationalism during the revolt of 1920, while Shia middle-class intellectuals helped to shape the Ba'ath Party's nationalist ideology in its formative years. This Iraqi-centric approach, combined with democracy, would automatically lead to a predominance of Shia politicians at the head of the state.[18] On the ground, however, the reality is more complex. Although Shias form the clear majority of the population, this majority is divided by geography and ideological arguments concerning the relationship between religion and the state.

There is a long-standing divide between the *ulama* and the wider Shia community in Iraq, exacerbated by the mass leftist politics of the 1950s and 1960s and the spread of secularism up to the 1980s. This mirrors an ideological divide in lay Shia life between those who support a broadly secular political platform that argues for greater equality and democracy, and those committed to the imposition of an Islamic state. In addition, a further division exists between the religious hierarchy that remained in Iraq under Saddam, and exiled groups in Iran and elsewhere. This division between exiled *ulama* and those who stayed was highlighted by the murder of Ayatollah Majid al-Khoei in Najaf shortly after the fall of the Ba'athist regime. Al-Khoei, a figure of significant influence amongst Shias globally, had spent many years in exile in London. After returning to Najaf following the downfall of the regime, he was murdered by a mob in the city's holiest shrine. The murder has been widely attributed to Sadr.

The Shia clerical establishment's power, coherence and influence in modern Iraq have been directly tied to the power of the state, and the incumbent regime's policies towards the *ulama*. Following the 1991 Gulf War and the drastic shortfall in resources imposed by sanctions, Saddam's regime allowed the Shia religious establishment to expand its charitable organisations, utilising donations from the Shia community abroad.[19] The regime's weakness was exploited by Ayatollah Muhammad Sadiq al-Sadr (Muqtada al Sadr's father) to build a large charitable network stretching from Baghdad to the south. As Sadr's influence increased, he married this social network to a powerful political message. His sermons, heard by thousands, were critical of Saddam, and called for Iranian-style rule by Islamic jurists. Following his murder by the government in 1999, his son Muqtada inherited both his father's radical, anti-establishment politics, and his charitable organisation. After the fall of the regime, Sadr used the charitable networks set up by his father as a system of local government, moving in to fill the post-invasion vacuum in the Sadr city area of Baghdad, where his militia imposed a rough-and-ready order. At one point, Sadr's organisation controlled as many as 90% of the mosques in this area.

Sadr has sought to organise those who lost most during the 1990s, namely poor, underemployed city-dwellers. This group has suffered from the occupation's failure to deliver order and sustained economic development. But Sadr is not just a rabble-rouser: his support extends into the lower ranks of the religious establishment, where he has found significant backing from young clerics, attracted by his youth, his lack of a religious education (younger clerics face long and arduous training) and the promise of a shortcut to moral and political influence.[20] Finally, within Najaf Sadr has capitalised on tensions between the large number of returning exiles, and those who feel threatened by their arrival.[21]

To rally this comparatively disparate group of supporters, Sadr has made use of a passionate rhetoric that merges militant Iraqi nationalism with a commitment to Islamic radicalism. In so doing, however, he has set himself against the traditional religious establishment. The pinnacle of this establishment is the *hawza 'ilmiyya* (the territory of learning), which is responsible for religious schools and institutions. The *hawza* is run by senior religious scholars or *marjas*, who have built up a personal coterie of students and followers. The *hawza* has traditionally been organised consensually, and is dependent on agreement amongst senior scholars in Najaf.[22] After the fall of Saddam's regime, large sections of the population turned to the *hawza* for guidance, but the diffuse and consensual nature of the organisation led to confusion, with different political groupings seeking to utilise its prestige and claiming to act in its name.

Out of this confusion, the 73-year-old Iranian-born Sistani emerged to become the most influential religious figure in the country. Since the fall of the regime Sistani, the most senior of the four Grand Ayatollahs in Najaf, has sought to institutionalise his position of authority within the *ulama*, and across society. In attempting to solidify his control over the *ulama*, Sistani has, however, faced several problems. His own position of influence has made him vulnerable to the political violence sweeping the country, and Sadr has issued veiled threats against him. Sistani has also become increasingly susceptible to local and international influence. His political philosophy expressly forbids the *ulama* from becoming directly involved in politics. This has reduced his appeal to those Iraqis who are alienated from the occupation, and Sadr has styled his own movement the radical *hawza*, contrasting it with the supposedly silent *hawza* of Sistani. Sistani is still struggling to control the religious establishment, while competing with Sadr for the support of the poorest and most disaffected sections of Iraqi society.

Two formal political parties, the Dawa Party and the Supreme Council for the Islamic Revolution in Iraq (SCIRI), are also competing for Shia support. However, both parties' attempts to build a significant political base in Iraq have been undermined by various factors. Shia political opinion has remained fluid, and has not coalesced around any one party or set of issues. Dawa and SCIRI have not developed an authentic indigenous platform and, by joining the Iraqi Governing Council, both became associated with an unpopular occupation and its failures. Sadr has attacked both SCIRI and Dawa as foreign imports closely tied to the US and Iran.

Dawa has promoted a brand of nationalist Islamism with a degree of success, but its history of internal division and ideological conflict has hampered efforts to build a national organisation. SCIRI, on the other hand, has struggled to escape its past as a vehicle of Iranian foreign policy. Formed in Tehran in 1982 during the Iran–Iraq war, it reflected the Iranian government's desire to unite the Iraqi Shia opposition against Saddam. Its dominant figure was the late Mohammed Baqir al Hakim, a scion of one of Iraq's major religious families. Hakim gained a great deal of his legitimacy from the actions of his father, Grand Ayatollah Mohsen al Hakim.[23] However, he never managed to develop a reputation for religious learning or authority, and on returning to Iraq left active politics to his brother, Abdul Aziz al Hakim. When Mohammed was murdered delivering Friday prayers in Najaf in late August 2003, his brother took over the movement.

The Kurdish north

The Kurdish enclave in the north of Iraq emerged in 1991 following the end of the Gulf War. From its inception, the enclave has offered an insight into what Iraq without Saddam might look like. The Kurds were eager to show that their bid for autonomy, if not outright independence, would be run along liberal and democratic lines. However, the lessons to be taken from the Kurdish experience are not straightforward, nor are they wholly positive.

In 1992, democratic elections were held across the enclave for a Kurdish regional parliament and government based in Arbil. The polls emphasised the polarised nature of Kurdish political life, with the Kurdish Democratic Party and the Patriotic Union of Kurdistan both securing roughly 50% of the votes cast. In an indication of tensions to come, the party leaders, Masoud Barazani and Jalal Talabani, refused to take a direct part in the coalition government formed after the elections, preferring to remain on the sidelines influencing events through proxies. Instead of building a government, each party concentrated on consolidating its regional support-base, creating two competing administrations and sabotaging any chance of a strong enclave-wide government. The two administrations were built to sustain party loyalty, not institutional capacity. The population experienced local government as an extension of political patronage, where loyalty was bought in the name of the party leaders.[24]

The tensions and rivalries between the PUK and KDP led to civil war within the enclave at the end of 1993. By 1994, PUK forces had seized Arbil, bringing to an end hopes for a united regional government. Regional powers began to be drawn into the conflict in order to gain some influence among the warring parties on their borders. Neighbouring states' secret services and armies operated with impunity, becoming key players in the struggle.

The conflict reached a peak in mid-1996. The KDP, fearing it was losing the battle with the PUK, appealed to Baghdad for military assistance, and at the end of August 30,000 Iraqi troops entered the enclave in tactical support of the KDP. With their help, the KDP temporarily captured Arbil, Suleimaniyah and the strategic town of Koi Sanjak. Some 39,000 refugees fled the area. The US finally intervened to broker an accommodation between the PUK and KDP, the Washington Accords, in September 1998. Today, each party runs a separate administration, raises its own taxes and maintains its own militia. This has retarded the growth of political pluralism and a free-market economy. Civil society and press freedom have flourished, but within very clear limits set and enforced by the KDP and PUK's security services. This process has extended into the economy, with the growth of a 'crony capitalism' designed to further entrench the KDP and PUK's grip on the enclave, and enrich their senior members.[25]

After Saddam's fall, both Barazani and Talabani realised that the only way to defend their own interests and the status quo in the north was to engage with politics in Baghdad, and negotiate on the national stage. To this end, both leaders became country-wide political figures. The negotiations surrounding the Transitional Administrative Law in the first few months of 2004 exemplified their tactics and goals, as well as the tensions involved in their approach. Aware that their autonomous positions and large militias gave them temporary leverage, both the KDP and PUK tried to secure the gains made by their parties over the 1990s by arguing for an ethnically based federalism. This was opposed by the Shia parties, which have long favoured a unitary state. The eventual compromise hammered out by Bremer entailed an agreement written into the transitional constitution that a vote by any three governorates could veto constitutional change. The Kurdish parties saw this as the minimum guarantee of their position within the Iraqi state.

When the guarantees of the Transitional Administrative Law were not included in UN Resolution 1546, which recognised Iraq's post-invasion international sovereignty, and the two parties were told that their representatives would hold neither the presidency nor the premiership, Barazani and Talabani threatened to 'refrain from participating in government' and to refuse to take part in the planned national elections. This was in effect a de facto threat of secession. This tactic, of taking part in national politics while using the threat of secession as the ultimate bargaining card, remains central to the KDP and PUK's post-election strategy. A series of policy issues, such as who controls the divided city of Kirkuk, the mechanism to allocate oil revenues and the structure for governing the country, remain 'trigger issues'. Kurdish negotiating teams indulge in brinkmanship, seeking to get the best possible deal by threatening the break-up of Iraq.

Arguably, the KDP and PUK leadership are not actually acting in an irresponsible manner. They are standing between the much more radical aspirations of the Kurdish population in the north and the constraints of national, regional and international politics. A generation of Kurds has reached adulthood since the enclave separated from Iraq. Their mother tongue is Kurdish, they have been immersed in a specifically Kurdish culture and schooled in the undoubted horrors that Baghdad once unleashed on their parents and grandparents. The Kurdish population has to be convinced of the utility of reunification with the rest of Iraq. For them, the achievements of the Kurdish enclave – comparative pluralism, stability and prosperity – far outweigh the political strife of its birth. At the present juncture, the dangers of full engagement with Iraqi politics are much greater than the potential benefits. This puts the Kurdish leadership in a difficult position. The ruling élites must sustain a degree of popularity and convince the population that a 'historic compromise' would be worth the risks involved.[26] A popular movement calling for a referendum on the future status of Kurdistan has highlighted the difficulties involved in this delicate balancing act. Started by Kurdish academics in 2004, it was quickly taken over by the KDP and PUK in an attempt to limit the potential damage of its results. Even so, the campaign attracted nearly two million supporters in a matter of weeks, showing the extent of popular aspirations for independence.

The position of the Kurdish enclave vis-à-vis the rest of Iraq has grown much stronger as first the Coalition Provisional Authority, then the Interim

Iraqi Government, failed to impose law and order. The Kurdish authorities have managed, with notable exceptions, to insulate the territory under their control from the violence sweeping the rest of the country. The administration built up since 1991, with all its imperfections, is still more coherent and efficient than the equivalent structures in the centre and south of the country. Continued failure to create a coherent administration and establish law and order in the rest of Iraq will only increase the enclave's de facto independence. Meanwhile, although the rivalry between the KDP and PUK has been temporarily set aside for the sake of wider questions of national politics, it has not gone away. Profound political divisions underlie the Kurds' strong desire for independence and their deep sense of Kurdish national identity.

Political mobilisation among Iraqi Sunnis

The political mobilisation of Iraq's Sunnis has been much slower and more decentralised than that of the country's other two main communities. Lacking both the centralised religious institutions of the Shia and the two dominant parties of the Kurds, Sunnis fear that the new order will result in their marginalisation and persecution. Political vehicles have had to be quickly built around the twin ideological concerns of nationalism and Islam.

The nature of this political mobilisation is a legacy of Ba'athist rule. Saddam's government worked hard to destroy any rival for collective organisation in Sunni society, targeting and co-opting its members. Some favoured members of the Sunni community became conduits for regime resources, and in return they were expected to provide the regime with intelligence about society. A good example of this process, and the way in which it transformed society, is the Ba'athist regime's relations with Iraqi 'tribes', and its attitude to 'tribalism'. On taking power the Ba'athists sought to accelerate what they saw as the disintegration of 'pre-modern' tribalism, which they viewed as linked to collaboration with British imperialism, backwardness and weakness. This process was driven forward by experiments in the collectivisation of land ownership in 1970, and the nationalisation of land in 1971.[27] With the rise of the Tikritis within the ruling élite, and the personalisation of power around Hasan al Bakr and Saddam, Ba'ath Party rule came to depend on the al-Bu Nasir tribe, and particularly the Beijat clan group and Majid family. As the Ba'ath Party sought to extend its totalitarian and patrimonial grip on society, it either co-opted tribal groupings that were useful to it, or broke those groupings that it regarded as a threat.[28]

This process reached its peak in the aftermath of the 1991 Gulf War. After 1991, Saddam curtailed the Ba'ath Party's role as a vehicle for societal mobilisation, but counterbalanced the decline in official institutions by developing a new network of patronage. In effect, Saddam decentralised responsibility for the provision of order to reinvigorated and recreated tribal networks and sheikhs. Following Saddam's fall, individuals such as the government-created sheikhs have, in the south and north of the country, either reached an accommodation with the new social forces unleashed by regime change, or they have been murdered or forced to flee. In areas where there was little organised resistance to Saddam, in Baghdad and the north-west of Iraq, their position is more ambiguous. Along with remnants of the security services, they have remained in place and are still associated with the old regime, albeit they are not the force they once were. Their existence has stunted the growth of alternative political structures and prevented the emergence of individuals capable of rallying popular support. They have used their old skills and networks to help organise the insurgency and fight the US occupation, and to combat the Iraqi government's attempts to extend its influence into areas they once controlled.

The political void at the heart of the Sunni community has been partially filled by Islamic nationalism, utilised by groups such as the re-formed Muslim Brotherhood and the Iraqi Islamic Party. However, it is indicative of the fractured nature of the polity that a coalition, not a single coherent party, the Association of Islamic Scholars, appears to have become most influential. Formed in 2003, the Association now claims to represent 6,000 mosques, nearly 80% of the national total. Its chief spokesperson, Dr Muthanna Harith al-Dhari, was educated at Cairo's prestigious Al Azha Islamic University, and taught in the Islamic Law Department of Baghdad University. His rhetoric mixes an austere Islamism with a powerful Iraqi nationalism that condemns those collaborating with the occupation.

Besides the Ba'ath Party itself, the Sunni community has lacked the collective organisation it needs to give it a coherent political voice. This void is still to be filled, but the mosque, Islam and Iraqi nationalism have proved to be the most powerful organisational and political forces available. This is not a homogenous approach. The Sunni Islamic movement is divided between different stances on religion: the Salafi and the Sufi, for example, hold different views on the use of violence in opposition to the occupation and the government. Nonetheless, the hostility felt by this section of Iraq's population towards the occupation, combined with profound political uncertainty and disorder, means that militant Islamism is likely to remain the predominant element in Sunni politics.

Conclusions

In the aftermath of regime change, a complex picture of the Iraqi polity has emerged. Opinion polling in a country that has recently emerged from dictatorship and is wracked with profound uncertainty and violence is bound to be an inexact science. Results from several polls in 2003 and 2004 have been somewhat contradictory, but do offer an indication of developments in public opinion.[29] During the 1990s, as sanctions devastated Iraqi society, there was a retreat into the certainties of religion. This trend was encouraged by the regime's *hamla imaniya*, or faith campaign, which relaxed the rules restricting religious observance and channelled state resources into mosque-building. This has left its mark on Iraqi society, particularly in the south and centre. In an April 2004 poll, 67% identified religion as the most important expression of their identity.[30] Only 1% of those questioned gave their tribe as the most important, and only 12% cited their ethnicity (66% of Kurds questioned cited ethnicity). The dominance of Islam as a marker of identity runs in tandem with strong support across the whole of Iraqi society for democracy, but not necessarily on a European or US model. Of 3,000 Iraqis polled in May 2004, three-quarters said that they 'want to live in a moderate Islamic democracy rather than a secular liberal one'.[31]

Nationalism and, indeed, the remnants of Ba'athist ideology appear to have resonance within the population, with the majority supporting a strong interventionist state. Polls carried out in February and May 2004 found support for a strong centralised state with Baghdad as its capital. The Iraqi Centre for Research and Strategic Studies found that 64.7% favoured 'a politically centralised, unitary state as opposed to a federation', with 67% saying that they wanted both fiscal and administrative centralisation. Oxford Research International polls in February, March and June found broadly similar views. In response to the question 'which structure should Iraq have in the future', 79% of respondents agreed with the statement 'one unified Iraq with a central government in Baghdad'. Although the figures differed according to the ethnic and regional background of those questioned, only 12% of Kurds, and 3.8% of all those surveyed, called for Iraq to be broken up into separate states.

What these figures indicate is that Iraqi public opinion is far more complicated than the caricature of three clearly delineated and mutually hostile communities divided by religion and ethnicity. There exists in Iraq today a strong sense of national identity and a widespread wish for a unitary state centred on Baghdad. However, opinion is clearly fluid, as are political identities and the bases for political mobilisation. It is therefore essential that care is taken now, as the nascent state institutions set about interacting with the population. If done incorrectly or on the basis of widely held misperceptions, the state could exacerbate sectarian and religious tensions. If, however, the state encourages a civic nationalism based on equal citizenship for all in a legal, rational, democratic state, then Iraqi politics could stabilise and the state could evolve into a legitimate and sustainable organisation.

The future of Iraq and the stability of the Greater Middle East

In the aftermath of the attacks on New York and Washington on 11 September 2001, President Bush's foreign-policy team naturally turned to the Middle East as the major problem facing the United States. The region provided the ideological and financial support for al-Qaeda. In Iran and Iraq, it also contained two of Bush's three 'axis of evil' states. The US administration's approach to the Middle East merged realist assumptions of immediate threat with a set of idealistic goals concerning the region's predicament.

The core of the Bush doctrine called for a radical reworking of the notion of state sovereignty. In return for the benefits bestowed on a sovereign state by the international community, Middle Eastern governments would now have to conform to a new set of rules, rejecting once and for all the use of terrorism as a tool of foreign policy, disavowing the development of weapons of mass destruction, and ensuring that terrorist groups were not harboured on their territory and did not use their banking systems. The military power and diplomatic capacity of the United States would be deployed to enforce these new demands on states across the developing world.

The United States' longer-term approach to the Middle East was much more ambitious, if not idealistic. To the White House, in the aftermath of 9/11, the Middle East appeared to be an area untouched by the positive changes unleashed at the end of the Cold War. The comparative domestic and international autonomy of states in the Middle East was identified as the source of this problem. Since independence, Middle Eastern oil-producing states had gradually increased their autonomy from their own people, and from the international system. This process was dramatically accelerated by the oil price rises of 1973–74. Oil-rich states could, in effect, demobilise the political aspirations of their societies by generous welfare spending, by not levying taxes and by imposing political quiescence. This autonomy from domestic and international society spread to the non-oil-producing states of the region, either as recipients of aid from the Gulf states, or as exporters of cheap labour.[1] With states able to suppress violently or financially co-opt secular dissent, the mosque and Islamic charitable organisations became the only sections of civil society that had not been bought or broken by dictatorial regimes. It is hardly surprising, then, that rising resentment took a religious form. From this grew the appeal of al-Qaeda.

Both the realist aims of the Bush doctrine and the White House's idealistic and transformative agenda were brought together in regime change in Iraq. The removal of Saddam would be the key to 'unlock' the Middle East. It would also eliminate a rogue state that had defied the international community for over a decade. By invading Iraq and deposing Saddam, Bush would be signalling that the post-9/11 demands of the United States must be complied with, or its military capacity would be deployed. Releasing the Iraqi population from 35 years of Ba'athist rule would also deliver a much larger objective. Post-Ba'athist Iraq would be reformed along neo-liberal lines. The role and size of state institutions would be greatly reduced, with private enterprise and international finance taking over. A democratic, prosperous Iraq, thriving under neo-liberal policy prescriptions, would lead by example, giving rise to social and economic changes which would transform the whole area.

However, the aftermath of regime change has proved to be much more difficult than anticipated. The military task of defeating the Ba'athist regime was relatively straightforward, but the political task has been complex, unpredictable and costly. With the collapse of Iraq's governing institutions in April 2003, the political mission of reforming the state was transformed into an exercise in state-building. State-building involves a three-stage process: order must be reimposed, the administrative capacity of the government rebuilt and sustainable economic development put in place.[2] Two years after the change in regime, there is little indication that the US military and its indigenous partner, the new Iraqi government, are any closer to completing the first stage in this process. There is a security vacuum in Iraq, with the institutions of law and order lacking the strength to guarantee stability in Baghdad, let alone across the country as a whole.

Against a background of violence and instability, the goals of Bush's foreign policy have been placed in doubt. The new government desperately needs both legitimacy and administrative capacity. By delivering 275 elected members to the new assembly, the January vote has given the new government a basis from which to build country-wide legitimacy. However, this is far from guaranteed. The assembly and its members will be involved in detailed and somewhat obscure negotiations about the new constitution. The danger is that those elected, shut away in the heavily fortified 'green zone' arguing about the legal structures of government, will lose touch with the hopes and expectations of those who elected them. A slow, post-election political demobilisation of the Iraqi people would increase the disappointment and alienation that came to dominate Iraq in the months after the regime fell. For the government to build on the success of the elections, it needs to put a great deal of time and effort into creating institutional links with Iraqi society. This should involve the basics of state-building, recreating a nationwide civil service linking the country to the government in Baghdad. Political parties, emboldened by their electoral success, should set about building national party machines, with local activists and offices explaining the policies being developed in Baghdad. In return, these party machines would feed back to the green zone the opinions, demands and hopes of the population at large. This would create a much-needed bridge between the government and its population.

Of more immediate importance will be the new government's ability to control the country. By January 2005, US forces had set themselves the target of training several divisions of the Iraqi army, as well as 50 or more battalions of the Iraqi National Guard.[3] The issue, however, is not just a matter of numbers of troops, hastily trained and rapidly deployed. To be successful, these new forces will have to become a visible testament to the new state's capacity to control the country. They would incrementally replace the US Army, and would be accepted by the population at large as the efficient and legitimate arm of a new Iraqi state. There is little sign that this is happening at the speed aimed for by the US military.

A realistic timetable for such a major and extended exercise in recruitment, training and institution-building would be at least five years. The lack of law and order would still dominate the everyday lives of Iraq's population while this process was unfolding. Against this background, a diplomatic solution to politically motivated violence is essential. This would involve drawing the political representatives of the insurgency into discussions about trading in their weapons and partaking in the democratic process. The elections were boycotted by a significant section of the

Iraqi population, who felt, through a mixture of fear and alienation, that they could not take part. If the new government does not manage to reach out to those sections of Iraqi society that already feel excluded from Iraqi politics, it will be increasingly difficult to find a diplomatic, and hence sustainable, solution to the insurgency.

Failure to impose order on Iraq, the continuing deaths of American soldiers and the continued commitment of troops will further undermine Washington's ability to project power across the region. Instead of regime change increasing US influence in the Middle East, prolonged involvement in Iraq will make it vulnerable to neighbouring states' ruling élites – the very people the Bush doctrine sought to constrain, if not remove.

Saudi Arabia, Washington's key ally in the region, but also the birthplace of Osama bin Laden and 15 of the 19 September 2001 hijackers, highlights the tension in policy between stability and reform. As a result of the scrutiny focused on the kingdom in the aftermath of 9/11, Crown Prince Abdullah launched a 'national dialogue' on the extent and pace of political change. This has resulted in a timetable for countrywide municipal elections, the first since the 1960s. These are to take place in a three-stage process, starting with partial local elections. However, the strict limits of this process have been highlighted by the continued persecution of Saudi liberals, with the arrest and imprisonment of prominent democracy activists. Reform could also be limited by an upsurge in radical Islamist violence. A small-scale campaign of bombing, which killed six Western workers between November 2000 and February 2003, escalated in November 2003, with the suicide bombing of a foreign workers' compound in Riyadh. In May 2004, Islamic radicals once again increased the scope of violence with attacks in the Red Sea oil centre of Yanbu, an attack on an oil compound in al Khobar, and finally the beheading of an American technician, Paul Johnson, in Riyadh.

A link between the invasion of Iraq in March 2003 and the increase in violence in Saudi Arabia has clearly been established. Saleh Awfi, the 33-year-old who was proclaimed head of al-Qaeda in the Arabian peninsula in July 2004, gained his military experience fighting US forces in Iraq in 2003 and 2004. Othman Amri, nineteenth on the Saudi government's most-wanted list, surrendered to the authorities in June 2004 after spending the previous 12 months fighting in Iraq. The group responsible for Johnson's beheading deliberately took the name the Falluja Brigade to draw a direct parallel between its use of violence in Saudi Arabia and the ongoing insurgency in Iraq. The campaign of violence in Saudi Arabia not only highlights the comparative weakness of the Saudi security forces and the porous nature of the borders between the kingdom and Iraq, but also the increased regional cooperation between groups seeking to drive the US out of the Middle East.

Although not included in Bush's 'axis of evil' speech, the Syrian regime of Bashar al Asad exhibits many of the traits that were the express targets of Bush's Middle East policy. The Syrian governing élite has historically striven to increase its autonomy from society, using a combination of populist rhetoric and coercion to control its population. In addition, it has supported radical Palestinian groups to further its own foreign-policy goals. The US administration's suspicions appeared to be confirmed when Rumsfeld and other senior officials accused Damascus of supporting Saddam's regime during the war.[4]

In the wake of the United States' swift military victory, Syria was forced to reach an accommodation with Washington. US Secretary of State Colin Powell travelled to Damascus in May 2003 with a set of specific demands. On wider Middle East issues, Syria agreed to reduce its support for radical Palestinian groups, closing down their press offices in Damascus and forcing them to lower their public profile. On specific Iraqi issues, Damascus repatriated the assets of the former regime and returned some former high-ranking personnel who had sought refuge in the country. However, as the situation in Iraq deteriorated Syria's position became ambiguous. Asad's regime claimed that it had sealed the border, and was not allowing Syrian and foreign fighters to cross into Iraq. But evidence in support of this proved mixed, indicating either that Damascus had difficulty in controlling its frontiers, or that it was quietly seeking a degree of leverage over the unfolding situation in Iraq. In an attempt to exert greater influence over Asad, Washington imposed sanctions at the end of 2003, through the Syrian Accountability and Lebanese Sovereignty Act. The murder of ex-Prime Minister Rafik Hariri in Beirut on 14 February 2004 triggered an upsurge in anti-Syrian activism. This forced the Syrian government to agree to a staged withdrawal of its security personnel from Lebanon.

It is in its relations with Iran that the United States has been confronted with the greatest contradiction between its foreign-policy aims and the difficulties it faces in Iraq. As one of Bush's 'axis of evil' states, the actions of the Iranian government bring together all of Washington's major regional concerns. Decision-making in Tehran is divided between the conservative inheritors of Ayatollah Khomeini's revolution and the liberal wing of the religious hierarchy, which is trying to meet demands from within Iranian society for greater democratic freedom. This struggle came to a head in the parliamentary elections of 2004. In what amounted to a constitutional coup, the conservatives banned 2,600 potential candidates from standing, thereby securing their domination of the Iranian parliament. Meanwhile, Iran's programme of uranium enrichment threatens to place it in conflict with the international community. The censure of the International Atomic Energy Agency has not forced it to abandon its programme.

When Saddam was overthrown, the Iranian government clearly felt vulnerable to US military power, and took steps to find an accommodation with Washington. However, as the situation in Iraq has deteriorated, the Iranian position has hardened. After an eight-year war, and given that the two countries share a long and porous border, there is no doubt that Iran has legitimate foreign-policy interests in Iraq. Iran has invested time and money in supporting one of the main Iraqi Shia parties, the Dawa Party, and created the other, the SCIRI, to increase its influence. To this end, Tehran encouraged Iran's commercial sector to strengthen trade links, and has increased the numbers of pilgrims and non-governmental charities operating in the south of Iraq. However, it is not economic or religious activity that has caused most concern. The main worry is the activity and intentions of Iranian government employees in Iraq.

Key Iraqi Shia religious figures interviewed in the spring of 2004 expressed active concern about Iranian intelligence personnel operating in Najaf. They argued that the level of this activity directly constrained the conduct and public statements of senior Shia figures.[5] Although the Iraqi defence minister has labelled Iran the country's 'first enemy', there is no direct evidence that the Iranian government is supporting or even encouraging the violence that has destabilised the country. Instead, the evidence points to a longer-term strategy to increase its capacity to influence events in Iraq. The danger is that, as Iran heads towards a confrontation with the international community over nuclear proliferation, Tehran will be tempted to use its networks of influence in Iraq as leverage. The Iranian government has developed the ability to further destabilise Iraq, and may do so if it feels threatened by the United States and the international community.

Iran and Syria both felt vulnerable after regime change. The logic of the Bush doctrine meant that increased US power in the Middle East would constrain both states' domestic and regional authority. When it looked like the US had triumphed in Iraq, both Damascus and Tehran felt that they had little choice but to conform to new regional realities. Cooperation was offered in the hope that the more radical aspects of the Bush doctrine could be tempered. As the law and order situation in Iraq worsened, Iran and Syria's leverage increased. For political, socio-cultural, historical and geographical reasons, Damascus and Tehran have influence over the key players trying to undermine US attempts at state-building in Iraq. Both have been careful not to overtly destabilise Iraq or to be caught offering ideological or material support to the insurgency. However, both hope that US foreign policy-makers will come to realise the logic of the situation, and agree to negotiate directly with the Syrian and Iranian regimes. This would engage these regimes in helping to stabilise Iraq in return for de facto pledges by the Bush administration not to interfere in their domestic politics. The danger is that, if such an understanding is not brokered, and if Iran's confrontation with the international community continues, Iraq will become an arena in which regional powers use violence to further their own foreign-policy aims.

In choosing regime change in Iraq as a core foreign-policy goal, the US administration assumed that a swift victory would make its wider aims more attainable. Its leverage in Tehran, Damascus and even Riyadh would be greater once Saddam had been removed and a pro-US government installed. However, the outcome has greatly differed from Washington's expectations. Iraq since April 2003 has become a magnet for radical Islamists seeking to fight US troops where they are at their most vulnerable. The task of stabilising Iraq and creating a viable government will take years. Meanwhile, Washington's influence in the region has been constrained. A necessary part of any solution to the violence and instability in post-Saddam Iraq is for Washington to take a more pragmatic and less adversarial approach to Iraq's neighbours, whose influence and long-term interest in Iraq will endure beyond the departure of the last American soldier.

Acknowledgements

This Adelphi Paper was largely researched and written while I was a Senior Research Fellow at the UK Economic and Social Research Council (ESRC) Centre for the Study of Globalisation and Regionalisation, University of Warwick. I would like to thank the director, Richard Higgott, and all the staff for their assistance. I would also like to thank all those at the IISS who contributed to the paper's research and writing, especially the production staff, Ayse Abdullah and Matthew Foley. Raad Al Kadiri, Clare Day, Tim Huxley, Steven Simon, Gary Samore, and Hilary Synott carefully read earlier drafts and made many useful suggestions. I would also like to thank Chris Isham, Carlo Brillarelli and Karin Weinberg at ABC TV for facilitating one of my research trips to Baghdad. Most importantly I would like to thank the many people who have taken the time to help me understand Iraqi politics. These include Khair El-Din Haseeb, Faleh Jabar, Raad Al Kadiri, Zuhair Al Kadiri, Isam Al Khafaji, Peter Sluglett, Gareth Stansfield, Charles Tripp, Sami Zubaida and numerous others whose names cannot be mentioned.

Notes

Introduction

[1] Toby Dodge and Steven Simon, 'Introduction', in *Iraq at the Crossroads: State and Society in the Shadow of Regime Change* (Oxford: Oxford University Press for the IISS, 2003), p. 11.

[2] See Bob Woodward's description of the National Security Council meeting on 12 September 2001 in *Bush at War* (New York: Simon and Schuster, 2002), pp. 43, 48.

[3] See the President's State of the Union Address, the United States Capitol, Washington DC, 29 January 2002.

[4] Robert S. Litwak, 'The New Calculus of Pre-emption', *Survival*, vol. 44, no. 4, Winter 2002–2003; and *The National Security Strategy of the United States of America*, September 2002, http://www.whitehouse.gov/nsc/nss.html. This was made even more explicit in the President's 2003 State of the Union address: 'Today, the gravest danger in the war on terror, the gravest danger facing America and the world, is outlaw regimes that seek and possess nuclear, chemical, and biological weapons. These regimes could use such weapons for blackmail, terror and mass murder. They could also give or sell those weapons to terrorist allies,

who would use them without the least hesitation'.

5   Remarks by Bush at the 2002 Graduation Exercise of the United States Military Academy West Point, New York, 1 June 2002; *The National Security Strategy of the United States of America*, pp. 1–2; Richard N. Haass, Director, Policy Planning Staff, 'The 2002 Arthur Ross Lecture, Remarks to the Foreign Policy Association New York', 22 April 2002; and G. John Ikenberry, 'America's Imperial Ambition', *Foreign Affairs*, September–October 2002, p. 52.

6   Nicholas Leman, 'After Iraq: The Plan to Remake the Middle East', *The New Yorker*, 17 February 2003.

7   Toby Dodge, 'Bringing the Bourgeoisie Back In: Globalisation and the Birth of Liberal Authoritarianism in the Middle East', in *Globalisation and the Middle East: Islam, Economics, Culture and Politics*

(London and Washington DC: RIIA and the Brookings Institution, 2002).

8   'President Discusses the Future of Iraq at the American Enterprise Institute', Washington Hilton Hotel, Washington DC, 26 February 2003.

9   On post-Cold War interventions see James Dobbins et al., *America's Role in Nation-Building: From Germany to Iraq*, RAND, 2003, http://www.rand.org/publications/MR/MR1753/MR1753.pref.pdf.

10 Lakhdar Brahimi, *Report of the Panel on United Nations Peace Operations*, UN document A/55/305S/2000/809; and *The Responsibility to Protect, Report of the International Commission on Intervention and State Sovereignty*, IDRC, 2001.

11 Steve Heder, 'Cambodia (1990–98): The Regime That Didn't Change', in Roger Gough (ed.), *Regime Change: It's Been Done Before*, (London: policyexchange, 2003).

Chapter One

1   For the classic definition see Max Weber, 'Politics as a Vocation', in H. H. Gerth and C. Wright Mills (eds), *From Max Weber: Essays in Sociology* (London: Routledge, 1991), pp. 78–79.

2   Simon Chesterman, *You, the People: The United Nations, Transitional Administrations, and State-building* (Oxford: Oxford University Press, 2004), pp. 100, 112.

3   Secretary of Defense Donald Rumsfeld was quoted at the time as saying 'Freedom's untidy. Free people are free to make mistakes and commit crimes and do bad things'.

4   Faleh A. Jabar, 'Post-Conflict Iraq, a Race for Stability, Reconstruction and Legitimacy', *United States Institute of Peace, Special Report 120*, May 2004, p. 6.

5   Dobbins et al., *America's Role in Nation-building*.

6   See Woodward, *Plan of Attack*, pp. 8, 36, 406; and Michael E. O'Hanlon and Adriana Lins de Albuquerque, *The Iraq Index*, http://www.brookings.org/iraqindex.

7   R. Beeston and T. Baldwin, 'Washington Hawks Under Fire for Ignoring Advice', *The Times*, 28 March 2003, p. 5.

8   'It's not too late for the Iraqi military to act with honour and protect your country'. President George W. Bush's address to the American people, 19 March 2003.

9   Quoted in 'Blair Orders Invasion Force This Month', *The Guardian*, 8 October 2002. This opinion was confirmed by discussions the author took part in at a very senior level in Whitehall in November 2002. See also Lawrence Freedman, quoted in Alan George, Raymond Whitaker and Andy McSmith, 'Revealed: The Meeting That Could Have Changed the History of Iraq', *The Independent on Sunday*, 17 October 2004.

10 Lawrence Freedman and Efraim Karsh, *The Gulf Conflict 1990–1991* (London: Faber and Faber, 1993), p. 307.

11 'In Nasiriyah Iraqi paramilitaries and elements of the 11th Regular Army division waged a week-long urban battle against

the Marine Corps' Task Force Tarawa, a reinforced three-battalion regimental-scale formation. In Samawah, Iraqi paramilitaries fought for a week against the Army's 3-7 Cavalry, the 3rd Brigade of the 3rd Infantry Division, and the 2nd Brigade of the 82nd Airborne Division in turn. In Najaf, urban warfare in and around the city centre continued for more than a week, tying down in series multiple brigades of American infantry.' Stephen Biddle *et al.*, 'Toppling Saddam: Iraq and American Military Transformation', US Army Strategic Studies Institute, 2004, pp. 6, 9, 10.

[12] Toby Dodge, 'Cake Walk, Coup or Urban Warfare: The Battle for Iraq', in Dodge and Simon (eds), *Iraq at the Crossroads*, p. 70.

[13] Ahmed S. Hashim, 'The Sunni Insurgency', *Middle East Institute Perspective*, 15 August 2003, p. 10.

[14] See, for example, US military spokesman Lt.-Col. George Krivo, quoted in Patrick E. Tyler and Ian Fisher, 'Occupiers, Villagers and an Ambush's Rubble', *International Herald Tribune*, 1 October 2003.

[15] Rory McCarthy, 'Death Toll for Week Tops 250 as Suicide Car Bomber Kills 13', *The Guardian*, 18 September 2004; and Edward Wong, 'Car Bombs Kill 26 in Baghdad and Mosul', *International Herald Tribune*, 5 October 2004.

[16] Brookings Institution, *Iraq Index: Tracking Variables of Reconstruction & Security in Post-Saddam Iraq*, www.brookings.edu/iraqindex, 12 March 2005.

[17] For discussion of the text see Dexter Filkins, 'Memo Urges Qaeda To Wage War in Iraq', *International Herald Tribune*, 10 February 2004; and Justin Huggler, 'Is This Man the Mastermind of the Massacres?', *Independent on Sunday*, 7 March 2004.

[18] See, for example, Abel Abdul Mehdi, an Iraqi Governing Council spokesman quoted in Rod Nordland, 'Thousands Attend the Funeral of Dozens Killed in the Karbala Explosions on March 2', *Newsweek*, 7 March 2004.

[19] This shift in the tempo and nature of attacks on coalition forces was exemplified by an attack on the governor's palace in Ramadi on 6 April 2004. Instead of striking coalition forces and then quickly retreating, insurgents dug in and engaged in a seven-hour firefight that killed 12 US Marines. Rory McCarthy, 'False Dawn of Peace Lost in Violent Storm', *The Guardian*, 8 April 2004.

[20] The US military estimates that 80% of all violence in Iraq is 'criminal in nature'. See Eric Schmitt and Thom Shanker, 'Estimates by US See More Rebels With Funds', *The Guardian*, 23 October 2004.

[21] Estimates taken from interviews carried out by the author with Iraqis politically active in the anti-occupation movement in early 2005.

[22] Dodge, 'Cake Walk, Coup or Urban Warfare'. See also Scott Ritter, 'Saddam's People Are Winning the War', *International Herald Tribune*, 23 July 2004; and Ali Ballout, 'Is Saddam Hussein's Post-War Plan Unfolding?', *The Daily Star*, Lebanon, 28 August 2003.

[23] This conclusion is supported by other work on the insurgency. See, for example, Ahmed S. Hashim, 'The Sunni Insurgency', *Middle East Institute Perspective*, 15 August 2003, p. 3.

[24] See the CPA's estimates, cited in Phyllis Bennis *et al.*, *A Failed 'Transition': The Mounting Cost of the Iraq War* (Washington DC: Institute for Policy Studies and Foreign Policy in Focus, 2004), p. 37. On the influence of de-Ba'athification on the intensity of the insurgency, see Jon Lee Anderson, 'Out On the Street', *The New Yorker*, 15 November 2004.

[25] This section of the paper is based on extensive interviews carried out by the author in the winter of 2004 and spring of 2005.

[26] Toby Dodge, 'US Intervention and Possible Iraqi Futures', *Survival*, vol. 45, no. 3, Autumn 2003, pp. 103–22; Charles Tripp, 'After Saddam', *Survival.*, vol. 44, no. 4, Winter 2002–2003, p. 26; and Charles Tripp, 'What Lurks in the Shadows?', *The Times Higher*, 18 October 2002, p. 17.

[27] Isam al-Khafaji, 'War as a Vehicle for the Rise and Decline of a State-Controlled Soci-

ety: The Case of Ba'athist Iraq', in Steven Heydemann (ed.), *War, Institutions, and Social Change in the Middle East* (Berkeley, CA: University of California Press, 2000).

28 This is based on interviews with senior Ba'ath Party officials who supervised the Islamic education of Ba'ath Party cadres.

29 Ayad Allawi showed himself to be keenly aware of this problem in a letter he sent to Bush in October 2004. See Peter J. Boyer, 'The Believer, Paul Wolfowitz Defends the War', *The New Yorker*, 1 November 2004.

30 This is based on interviews carried out in Baghdad in the aftermath of the fall of the regime.

31 Gareth Stansfield, 'The Kurdish Dilemma: The Golden Era Threatened', in Dodge and Simon (eds), *Iraq at the Crossroads*. On the complexity of Ansar al Islam's relations with al-Qaeda, see Jason Burke, *Al Qaeda: The True Story of Radical Islam* (London: Penguin, 2004), p. 11.

32 Woodward, *Plan of Attack*, p. 300. The veracity of this report has been frequently questioned.

33 See James Drummond, 'A Year After the Invasion the Spectre of Murderous Civil War Still Hangs over Iraq', *Financial Times*, 20 March 2004; Edward Wong, 'Mayhem in Iraq Is Starting To Look Like a Civil War', *The New York Times*, 5 December 2004; and Rory McCarthy and Qais al-Bishir, 'Gunmen Kill Deputy Chief of Baghdad Police', *The Guardian*, 11 January 2005.

34 Dexter Filkins, 'Iraqi Militias Are Said To Approve a Deal To Disband', *New York Times*, 8 June 2004.

35 On the plan itself, see Eric Schmitt and Thom Shanker, 'US Plans for Iraq Start

with Taming Insurgents', *New York Times*, 9 October 2004.

36 Jean Eaglesham and Charles Clover, 'UK Denies Troops for Iraq Will Help Bush Re-election', *Financial Times*, 18 October 2004.

37 Jackie Spinner, 'Insurgent Base Discovered in Falluja', *Washington Post*, 19 November 2004. The classified Marine Intelligence report was quoted in Eric Schmitt and Robert F. Worth, 'Marine Officers See Risk in Cut in Falluja Force', *New York Times*, 18 November 2004.

38 Farnaz Fassihi *et al.*, 'Initial Decisions in Iraq Continue To Haunt US as Instability Escalates', *Wall Street Journal Europe*, 19 April 2004.

39 *Iraq in Transition: Post Conflict Challenges and Opportunities*, Open Society Institute and the United Nations Foundation, 2004, p. 31.

40 Steve Negus, 'The Insurgency Intensifies', *Middle East Reports*, no. 232, Autumn 2004, p. 26.

41 *Iraq Index*, 17 November 2004.

42 See Robin Wright and Josh White, 'US Plans New Tax after Iraq elections', *Washington Post*, 23 January 2005.

43 Kim Sengupta, 'Onslaught on Samarra Escalates in "Dress Rehearsal" for Major Assault on Rebels', *Independent on Sunday*, 12 October 2004; Schmitt and Shanker, 'US Says Resistance in Iraq Up To 20,000'; and Kim Sengupta, 'Eight US Marines Killed in Fallujah Province While Air Strikes Intensify', *Independent on Sunday*, 31 October 2004.

44 Bruce Hoffman, *Insurgency and Counter Insurgency in Iraq* (Santa Monica, CA: RAND, June 2004), p. 16.

Chapter Two

1 Faleh A. Jadar, *Postconflict Iraq: A Race for Stability, Reconstruction and Legitimacy*, United States Institute of Peace Special Report, no. 120, May 2004, p. 14.

2 Michael Mann, 'The Autonomous Power of the State: Its Origins, Mechanisms and

Results', in Michael Mann, *States, War and Capitalism: Studies in Political Sociology* (Oxford: Blackwell, 1988).

3 Gianfranco Poggi, *The State: Its Nature, Development and Prospects* (Cambridge: Polity Press, 1990), p. 30.

4 Mann, 'The Autonomous Power of the State', p. 5.

5 Isam al-Khafaji, 'The Myth of Iraqi Exceptionalism', *Middle East Policy*, no. 4, October 2000, p. 68.

6 Charles Tripp, *A History of Iraq* (Cambridge: Cambridge University Press, 2000), pp. 205–206.

7 A visit to any government institution during the 1990s was a sobering event. In the middle of May 2001, the author secured an interview with a provincial governor in an area of southern Iraq where the government was feeling particularly vulnerable. On entering the building I had to step over a pool of raw sewage to reach his office. Clearly, the power of the state was not residing in this building.

8 Quoted in Michael Gordon, '"Catastrophic Success": The Strategy to Secure Iraq Did Not Foresee a 2nd War', *New York Times*, 19 October 2004.

9 'So massive was the looting that, just three days after the US secured the capital, computers were selling for as little as $35 in the thieves' market'. Mark Fineman, Robin Wright and Doyle McManus, 'Washington's Battle Plans, Preparing for War, Stumbling to Peace', *Los Angeles Times*, 18 July 2003.

10 See David L. Phillips, 'Listening to the Wrong Iraqi', *New York Times*, 20 September 2003.

11 Kanan Makiya and two other Iraqi exiles visited Bush in the White House in January 2003. They told him that US troops would be greeted with 'sweets and chocolate'. See George Packer, 'Kanan Makiya, Dreaming of Democracy', *New York Times Magazine*, 2 March 2003. This theme was also promoted by the influential Washington pundit Fouad Ajami, in 'Iraq and the Thief of Baghdad', *New York Times*, 19 May 2002. Ajami's predictions were in turn quoted by US Vice-President Dick Cheney in a speech in the summer of 2002.

12 Fineman, Wright and McManus, 'Washington's Battle Plans'; David Rieff, 'Blueprint for a Mess', *New York Times*

Magazine, 2 November 2003; and George Packer, 'Letter from Baghdad: War after War', *The New Yorker*, 24 November 2003.

13 Isam al Khafaji, 'A Few Days After: State and Society in a Post-Saddam Iraq', in Dodge and Simon (eds), *Iraq at the Crossroads*.

14 This finding was supported by an opinion poll carried out on 9 June 2004 by the Iraqi Centre for Research and Strategic Studies, which found that 'only 15.1% of Iraqis polled in Baghdad said that the political parties in Iraq represented their interests. Approximately 63% of those surveyed preferred a technocratic government, rather than one based upon political parties'. Puneet Talwar and Andrew Parasiliti, 108th Congress, 1st Session, Committee print, 'Iraq: Meeting the Challenge, Sharing the Burden, Staying the Course, A Trip Report to Members of the Committee on Foreign Relations, United States Senate', p. 9.

15 Interview, Baghdad, May 2003.

16 See International Crisis Group, 'Governing Iraq Middle East Report No. 17', Baghdad/Washington/Brussels, August 2003, p. 11.

17 The US organisers acknowledged that the meeting was 'not sufficiently representative to establish an interim authority'. See Jonathan Steele, 'Delegates Agree New Talks on Government', *The Guardian*, 29 April 2003.

18 These issues dominated the thinking of senior UN civil servants interviewed by the author in New York in May 2003. See Jonathan Steele, 'De Mello Knew Sovereignty, Not Security, Is the Issue', *The Guardian*, 21 August 2003; and Edward Mortimer, 'Iraq's Future Lies Beyond Conquest', *Financial Times*, 22 August 2003.

19 Rend Rahim Francke, 'Iraq Democracy Watch: On the Situation in Iraq', September 2003, http://www.iraqfoundation.org/news/2003/isept/26_democracy_watch.html, pp. 8–9.

20 Quoted in Robin Wright and Rajiv Chandrasekaban, 'US Ponders Alternatives to

Iraq Governing Council', *Washington Post*, 9 November 2003.

21 Daniel Williams, 'Iraqi Warns of Delay on Constitution Vote', *Washington Post*, 10 November 2003.

22 'Factions Tussle for Post of Iraqi President', *Financial Times*, 31 May 2004.

23 On the Brahimi plan, see 'Statement of the Special Adviser to the Secretary-General, Lakhdar Brahimi, to the Security Council on the Political Transition Process in Iraq', 27 April 2004; and 'Briefing of Special Adviser to UN Secretary-General, Lakhdar Brahimi to the Security Council on the Political Transition Process in Iraq', New York, 7 June 2004.

24 For a selection of this coverage, see http://www.iwpr.net/index.pl?iraq_ipm_index.html.

25 Roula Khalaf, Nicolas Pelham and James Drummond, 'UN Envoy Arrives in Baghdad as Storm Brews over Government', *Financial Times*, 6 May 2004.

26 On Brahimi's threats to resign see Polly Toynbee, 'Blair's Perversity Does Him Harm and Iraq No Good', *The Guardian*, 12 May 2004; for the unfolding of the process see Jonathan Steele, 'How Honest Broker Was Defeated – And With Him Hopes of Credibility', *The Guardian*, 3 June 2004.

27 Mark Turner, 'Poll Planning on Track But No Room for Hitches', *Financial Times*, 14 October 2004.

28 Edward Wong, 'Date Set for Iraq Elections, Violence Slows Registration', *New York Times*, 22 November 2004.

29 Walter Pincus, 'Iraqi Rules for Candidacy Spur Some US Concern', *Washington Post*, 6 November 2004.

30 See Rory McCarthy, 'Violence Will Not Stop Poll, Says UN official', *The Guardian*, 21 January 2005.

31 See John F. Burns and James Glanz, 'Iraqi Shiites Win, But Margin Is Less Than Projections', *New York Times*, 14 February 2005.

32 See Charles Clover, 'Seeking Votes: Iraq's Insurgents Consider Making Politics Their New Battleground', *Financial Times*, 21 October 2004.

33 Maina Ottaway, 'Don't Rig the Iraqi Election', *Washington Post*, 8 November 2004.

34 Charles Clover, 'Shia Look To Dominate Iraqi Parliament', *Financial Times*, 3 November 2004.

35 See Dexter Filkins, 'Shiites Rule Out Clerics in Top Iraqi Leadership', *New York Times*, 24 January 2005.

36 See Jonathan Steele, 'Beyond the Bullets, A New Constitution Is the Crucial Issue for This Democracy', *The Guardian*, 31 January 2005; and Brian Whitaker, 'Shunned Prime Minister Allawi Becomes Outsider', *The Guardian*, 14 February 2005.

37 See Steve Negus and Dhiya Rasan, 'Shia Group Reaches Out To Win Secular Voter', *Financial Times*, 27 January 2005; and Trudy Rubin, 'Some Iraqis Want US To Stay', *Philadelphia Inquirer*, 25 January 2005.

38 For examples, see 'Iraqi Police Drawn into Poll Contest as Gloves Come Off', *Financial Times*, 19 January 2005.

39 On electoral turn-out, see Anthony Shahid and Doug Struck, *The Washington Post*, 14 February 2005; Steve Negus, 'Shia Coalition Wins 48% of Iraqi Vote To End Sunni Domination', *Financial Times*, 14 February 2005; Dexter Filkins, 'Split Verdict in Iraqi Vote Sets Stage for Weak Government', *New York Times*, 14 February 2005; and Burns and Glanz, 'Iraqi Shiites Win'.

40 Stephen Krasner, *Sovereignty: Organized Hypocrisy* (Princeton, NJ: Princeton University Press, 1999), p. 12.

Chapter Three

1   This was the central reason for the failure of British attempts to build a stable state in Iraq from 1920 to 1932. Toby Dodge, *Inventing Iraq: The Failure of Nation Building and a History Denied* (New York and London: Columbia University Press and Hurst & Co., 2003), esp. pp. 83–100.

2   Quoted in Brendan O'Neill, 'Another Dodgy Dossier', *The Guardian*, 25 March 2004.

3   These figures are taken from the UN World Food Programme, the US Central Intelligence Agency and the World Bank. See http://www.worldbank.org/cgi-bin/sendoff.cgi?page=%2Fdata%2Fcountryda ta%2Fict%2Firq_ict.pdf and http://www.odci.gov/cia/publications/factbook/print/iz.html.

4   These figures are quoted in Samir al-Khalil, *Republic of Fear: Saddam's Iraq* (London: Hutchinson Radius, 1989), p. 215, who in turn refers to Gabriel Baer, *Population and Society in the Arab East* (London: Routledge & Kegan Paul, 1964).

5   See the CIA World Factbook, 2004.

6   For a short account of this argument see Leslie H. Gelb, 'Divide Iraq into Three States', *International Herald Tribune*, 26 November 2004. Peter W. Galbraith develops it at greater length in 'How To Get Out of Iraq', *New York Review of Books*, 13 May 2004. At over 200 pages, the argument's most detailed exposition is Liam Anderson and Gareth Stansfield, *The Future of Iraq: Dictatorship, Democracy or Division?* (New York: Palgrave MacMillan, 2004). Both Gelb and Galbraith have professional experience in the Balkans, and may be influenced by their understanding of the violent break-up of Yugoslavia in the mid-1990s.

7   For an excellent summary of the literature on this subject, see Nelson Kasfir, 'Explaining Ethnic Political Participation', in Atol Kholi (ed.), *The State and Development in the Third World* (Princeton, NJ: Princeton University Press, 1986). Also see David D. Laitin, *The Russian-Speaking Populations in the Near Abroad* (Ithaca, NY: Cornell University Press, 1998), pp. 13–21 and 325–29; and Joseph Rothchild, *Ethnopolitics: A Conceptual Framework* (New York: Columbia University Press, 1981).

8   Phebe Marr, 'Comments', *Middle East Policy*, no. 4, October 2000, p. 87.

9   Charles Tripp, 'Domestic Politics in Iraq: Saddam Hussein and the Autocrat's Fallacy', in Anoushiravan Ehteshami and Gerd Nonneman with Charles Tripp, *War and Peace in the Gulf: Domestic Politics and Regional Relations into the 1990s*, (Reading: Ithaca Press, 1991).

10 Toby Dodge, 'US Intervention and Possible Iraqi Futures', p. 109.

11 Al-Khafaji, 'The Myth of Iraqi Exceptionalism'.

12 Faleh A. Jabar, 'Sheikhs and Ideologues: Deconstruction and Reconstruction of Tribes under Patrimonial Totalitarianism in Iraq, 1968–1998', in Faleh A. Jabar and Hosham Dawod (eds), *Tribes and Power: Nationalism and Ethnicity in the Middle East* (London: Saqi, 2003), p. 89.

13 International Crisis Group, 'Governing Iraq Middle East Report No. 17', Baghdad/Washington/Brussels, August 2003, p. 1; and Jadar, *Postconflict Iraq*, p. 10.

14 Amatzia Baram, *Culture, History and Ideology in the Formation of Ba'thist Iraq, 1968–89* (New York: St. Martin's Press, 1991).

15 Faleh A. Jabar, *The Shi'ite Movement in Iraq* (London: Saqi, 2003), p. 254.

16 Faleh A. Jabar, 'The Iraqi Army and Anti-Army: Some Reflections on the Role of the Military', in Dodge and Simon (eds), *Iraq at the Crossroads*, p. 118.

17 Jabar, *The Shi'ite Movement in Iraq*, p. 37.

18 Pierre-Jean Luizard, 'The Iraqi Question from the Inside', *Middle East Report*, no. 193, March–April 1995, p. 19.

19 Faleh A. Jabar, 'Clerics, Tribes, Ideologues and Urban Dwellers in the South of Iraq: The Potential for Rebellion', in Dodge and Simon (eds), *Iraq at the Crossroads*, p. 170.

20 See Shi'ism: 'Varied Social Settings, Rival Centre of Power and Conflicting Visions', International Crisis Group Report, Part Two, Baghdad, 5–6 July 2003, expanded 12–15 July 2003, p. 8; and Jabar, *The Shi'ite Movement in Iraq*, p. 26.

21 International Crisis Group, 'Iraq's Shiites Under Occupation', Middle East Briefing, Baghdad/Brussels, 9 September 2003, p. 18.

22 *Ibid.*, pp. 8–9.

23 *Ibid.*

24 Michiel Leezenberg, 'Economy and Society in Iraqi Kurdistan: Fragile Institutions and Enduring Trends', in Dodge and Simon (eds), *Iraq at the Crossroads*, p. 151.

25 *Ibid.*

26 International Crisis Group, 'Iraq's Kurds: Towards an Historic Compromise?', Brussels/Amman, 8 April 2004.

27 Tripp, *A History of Iraq*, pp. 205–206.

28 Jabar, 'Sheikhs and Ideologues', pp. 69–101; and Amatzia Baram, 'Neo-Tribalism in Iraq: Saddam Hussein's Tribal Policies 1991–99', *International Journal of Middle Eastern Studies*, 29 (1997), pp. 1–31.

29 On the difficulties of opinion polling in Iraq see O'Neill, 'Another Dodgy Dossier'. On the misuse of opinion polls see James Zogby, 'Bend It Like Cheney', *The Guardian*, 29 October 2003.

30 The poll was commissioned by USA Today and CNN. It questioned 3,444 people across Iraq between 22 March and 2 April 2004. The confessional breakdown was: Shiite 73%, Sunni 76% and Kurd 33%.

31 See www.bridgesconsortium.org.

Conclusion

1 Toby Dodge and Richard Higgott, 'Globalisation and Its Discontents: The Theory and Practice of Change in the Middle East', in *Globalisation and the Middle East*, pp. 13–35.

2 See, for example, Francis Fukuyama, *State-Building: Governance and World Order in the Twenty-First Century* (London: Profile, 2004), p. 135; and Amitai Etzioni, 'A Self-Restrained Approach to Nation-Building by Foreign Powers', *International Affairs* vol. 80, no. 1, 2004, pp. 1 and 11.

3 This is broadly Paul Wolfowitz's vision of how Iraq will progress over the next 18 months. See Boyer, 'The Believer'.

4 Volker Perthes, *Syria Under Bashar al-Asad: Modernisation and the Limits of Change*, Adelphi Paper 366 (Oxford: Oxford University Press for the IISS, 2004), p. 50.

5 Professor Larry Diamond, a senior adviser to the Coalition Provisional Authority in Iraq in 2004, estimates the number of Iranian government personnel in Iraq to be as high as 14,000. See 'The Testimony of Larry Diamond to the Senate Foreign Relations Committee, Washington DC, May 19, 2004', p. 11. Senior British diplomats put the figure in the low thousands.